THE SOLUTIONS FACTORY

The Solutions Factory

A Consultant's Handbook for Problem-solving

Arun Maira

PENGUIN
VIKING

An imprint of Penguin Random House

VIKING

USA | Canada | UK | Ireland | Australia
New Zealand | India | South Africa | China

Viking is part of the Penguin Random House group of companies
whose addresses can be found at global.penguinrandomhouse.com

Published by Penguin Random House India Pvt. Ltd
4th Floor, Capital Tower 1, MG Road,
Gurugram 122 002, Haryana, India

First published in Viking by Penguin Random House India 2021

ISBN 9780670095483

Typeset in Adobe Garamond Pro by Manipal Technologies Limited, Manipal
Printed at Replika Press Pvt. Ltd, India

www.penguin.co.in

CONTENTS

PREFACE

Business schools provide a fast elevator for students who want to earn high salaries quickly. Management consulting provides them with a bridge high up in the sky between the world of education and the world of business.

The Petronas Twin Towers in Kuala Lumpur was the tallest building in the world from 1998 to 2004 when it was overshadowed by another building, Taipei 101. However, the Petronas Towers remain the tallest twin towers in the world. The two towers are connected by a double-decker skybridge 170 metres above ground, which is the highest two-storey bridge in the world. It enables people at the uppermost levels of the towers to cross over without bothering to come down to the ground at all.

In the world of business, one tower is the education tower with business schools at the top, the other is the corporate tower with C-suites of the largest multinational firms at its apex. The best students from the best business schools are picked by marquee international consulting companies, such as McKinsey & Company, Boston Consulting Group, and

Bain & Company. They cross the skybridge frequently to support the firms' partners in advising chief executive officers (CEOs) and chief experience officers (CXOs) in their offices at the top of the other tower. While the young consultants, though very well paid, earn much less than their partners and their partners' clients, they stick around to participate in the world of ideas high up there at a very young age. It is a great attraction for them to observe how important business decisions are made.

Big business ideas began to dominate the world since the 1990s, with the collapse of the Soviet Union and, with it, a dissipation of ideological opposition to the sway of private capital in the governance of economies. 'Government is not the solution to our problem, government is the problem,' Ronald Reagan had declared. Nevertheless, everywhere there is a government, including in the USA where Ronald Reagan himself was perched atop one. The problem is that government is not efficient, he said. It wastes resources, whereas the private sector, with its drive for efficiency and profits, knows how to use public resources better. Thus, with the spread of ideas of the 'Washington Consensus' since 1990, a global drive has gathered momentum to sell off government-owned companies, privatize public services and apply business management methods to governments' own ministries. This drive has expanded the market for management consultants beyond business into government. With that, opportunities for young management consultants to serve public causes has expanded further, making careers in management consulting even more attractive.

The incestuous mingling of the worlds of businesses, governments and management consultants has become increasingly visible every winter at the World Economic Forum (WEF) in the ski resort of Davos up in the Swiss Alps. Meanwhile, non-governmental organizations (NGOs), and representatives of environmental and human rights movements gather more humbly at sea level at Porto Alegre in Brazil at the World Social Forum (WSF). The distance between the amount of wealth earned by those on top and those sweating below has increased fast. In fact, every year, Oxfam presents a report to the WEF about how much richer the rich have become. At the last count in 2020, less than fifty persons in the world owned as much wealth as half of the world's population, i.e. over three and a half billion persons!

I came into the world of management consulting from 'the other tower'—the world of business corporations, having taken twenty-five years, in a slow elevator, to get to the skybridge of consultancy. When I stepped on to it, I found it was crowded with young consultants from management schools, who had come up very fast through the other tower.

The young consultants and I often saw the world through different lenses. When I began to consult in the USA, as a rookie in consulting, I earned about the same amount as the young consultants who were hired from the best business schools. When I had been consulting for less than two years and had established the value of my experience for CXOs in companies, a young colleague asked me a personal question, comparing my earnings with those of the young consultants,

'How come you are not rich if you are so good?' he asked. I sensed he was not sure whether I could be good, if I was not rich.

I believe that my long experience of working at lower levels in the organizations, close to the people on the ground, has given me a more grounded perspective of the worlds of business and consulting. In the twenty years of consulting, I wrote five books on my reflections on business transformation, the future of India and the future of democracy. The fifth, *Transforming Capitalism: Business Leadership to Improve the World for Everyone,* was published in 2008 just before I hung up my boots as the chairman of the Boston Consulting Group (India) Private Ltd.

Lately, objections from the masses against the go-go capitalism that became ascendant since the 1990s with its philosophy 'business of business is only business', and which has infected government policies too, have raised questions about the ethics of business.

During my twenty years with international consulting companies, I visited business schools often—to teach, to recruit young people for jobs, and even as a member of the boards of governance of some schools. Business schools which provide managers for businesses, and where professors provide ideas for business management, have come under pressure lately to teach ethics and not just efficiency, the value of equity and not just the value of profit. The Indian Institute of Management Calcutta (IIMC) had invited me to be the chief guest at its annual convocation in 2008 to speak about the value-based ideas in my book, *Transforming Capitalism:*

Business Leadership to Improve the World for Everyone, to its graduating students, most of whom had already been recruited by management consulting companies and blue-chip corporations.

In 2009, I was invited by the Prime Minister of India to join the Planning Commission. I was privileged to sit in an advisory capacity in a prominent place behind the prime minister and his cabinet to witness the issues being discussed and implemented across vast and incredible India—foreign trade and investments, the ravaging of the environment, the persistence of poverty, increasing inequality and the raucous contentions amongst stakeholders.

There was a pressure on the government to make it easier for business to do business and to move India higher up in the World Bank's 'ease of doing business' rankings to attract more foreign investments. There was also the pressure from civil society organizations (CSOs) for the government to focus much more on 'ease of living' for people at the bottom of the pyramid, rather than the ease of making profits for businesses at the top.

Young Indians today are sensitive to the world around them. Now, more graduates from the best business schools want to work in the not-for-profit world. They may earn less, they know; but they hope they will be able to make the world better.

The world is changing, and so is the world of business, of business schools and management consulting. I am often asked by young people whether they should join a consulting company where they will earn much more, or venture into the not-for-profit world. They want to know what is expected of them to succeed as consultants. I ask them to reflect on the purpose of their lives and to consider why and for whom they want to do good. Is it for themselves or for those who have less opportunities and privileges than they have?

For whose benefit should I use my talent is an ethical question. Ethics cannot be taught in a classroom. An ethical orientation is learnt by facing up to dilemmas. The question of whether the purpose of the action is to produce gain for oneself (consistent with the principle of 'rational self-interest' which is at the foundation of mainstream economics) or to help others is a complex one. As complex is the dilemma of who, other than oneself, should gain more from one's selfless actions, because consequences of actions are not evenly distributed—there are often losers as there are gainers. There are no formulae for this. Valuations can be computed; values cannot. We learn to take ethical decisions by experience and deep reflection.

Not only do young people ask me to guide them in making choices to become a consultant or not, but also many older persons who are choosing to become consultants (or coaches to others) later in their career, ask me how they can do better.

I have chosen to describe what consultants do by telling stories about consultants' dilemmas. Stories are a better way to communicate intangible values than numbers and prescriptions. All the stories in this book are personal stories about what I experienced as a consultant, what I learnt and the choices I made. I hope these stories will provide some useful insights for anyone, young or old, who wants to be a consultant.

PURPOSE AND ETHICS

WHO IS A CONSULTANT?

Consultants are of many kinds and consulting companies provide manifold services. If you want to be a consultant, be sure you know what you really want to do before taking the plunge into consulting.

When bright young people, graduating from the best universities, ask me for advice on their careers, they often ask whether they should join a consulting company. They expect that I can guide them because I have worked in senior positions with well-known international management consulting companies, both in the USA and in India, for twenty years, officially retiring from the profession as the chairman of the Boston Consulting Group (India) in 2008.

These young persons in their twenties have their whole working life before them. I was forty-five when I joined a consulting company, with half my working life behind me. They have a choice whether to join a consulting company or not; I had no option at that time.

When I graduated in 1964, I had joined the Tata Administrative Services. The only other option I had considered seriously was to join the government in the Indian Administrative Service. There were no management consulting companies in the country then. Even the Indian Institutes of Management were just being established. I learnt management by 'rubbing my nose on the shop floor', heeding the advice of my mentor Sumant Moolgaokar, vice chairman of the Tata Group, and by being thrown into real-life-management challenges. It had been quite exhilarating.

In 1989, it had become necessary for me to live and work in the United States due to a combination of family needs including the health condition of one of my children. It was not easy to move from India as I had been doing well at very senior levels in the Tata Group, at a young age. The Tatas could not transfer me to one of their set-ups in the USA because there was nothing worthwhile for me to do there at that time, as Mr J.R.D. Tata, the group chairman, had explained to me. However, he did want to help so he offered me a sabbatical from the Tatas and suggested I apply for a job in a consulting company in the USA where they might pay me well and I would also learn how companies in other countries were managed, which would be very valuable knowledge for me, as well as for the Tatas, when I would return to the group.

The problem though was, as Mr Tata pointed out, it was unlikely that US management consulting companies would recruit a forty-five-year-old manager of an Indian company who did not even have a management degree. What value could such a consultant provide to their clients in the USA, many of which were amongst the world's most successful companies and some of their stories were case studies in the best business schools? As a long shot, he suggested I approach Arthur D. Little Inc. (ADL), the world's oldest consulting company, founded in 1886, headquartered in Cambridge, Massachusetts.

Mr Tata had been impressed by ADL. He had seen them at work as consultants to the Government of India on a national science policy in the 1950s when he was invited by the government to join the committee because the Tata Group had a long history of supporting science institutions in India, such as the Indian Institute of Science in Bangalore, founded in 1909, which remains one of the highest ranked Indian educational institutions.

Mr Tata gave me a letter of recommendation to ADL with which I approached them. They hired me.

I reported for duty at ADL's campus in Acorn Park in Cambridge, Massachusetts. An ADL custom was to induct all new employees together in the week they joined the company. In the induction, apart from me, there was a woman who had joined as a secretary and a lab assistant who had joined one of ADL's large scientific labs nestled in its sprawling campus. The ADL consultant who was inducting the three of us said that it was a historic day because on that very day an ADL consultant was working on every continent in the world, including Antarctica! He also told us that the most scientific experiments by any private company to find place in the National Aeronautics and Space Administration (NASA) satellite circling the world then belonged to ADL.

What do consultants do? What was the ADL consultant doing in frozen, uninhabited Antarctica? He was in an oceanographic research vessel conducting research in climate change. Meanwhile, the consultants in Africa were advising governments on their agricultural and industrial policies, while the consultants in the Americas and Europe were mostly advising businesses—on strategies, operations improvements and research and development (R&D)—as well as consulting with governments. NASA was a client of ADL as was General Motors (GM). In fact, ADL had assisted GM to establish its first R&D laboratories in 1911.

Now I could understand why the Government of India had engaged ADL to develop a science policy for India. But I was concerned how I, a self-taught manager from India, would fit into the world of ADL and its clients.

Unlike the other management consulting companies—the most successful of which was McKinsey—that concentrated on hiring the best of the best students directly from management schools, ADL quite often took in 'lateral hires' with previous work experience. The other companies were averse to hiring 'laterals' because they wanted to develop their own consultants to fit into their own cultures and to teach them their ways of consulting. They were quite territorial about their unique cultures and consulting methods.

ADL expected me to figure out by myself how an Indian manager, who had 'rubbed his nose on Indian shop floors' for years and had sold Indian trucks and buses in foreign markets, would be valuable to companies like GM and other ADL clients that had a choice to hire the best management consultants from McKinsey and other consulting companies staffed with the brightest graduates from the finest US business schools.

I did quite well though. Ten years later I was ready to return to India; the family's needs had been met and both the children were well. I wanted to be back home to apply what I had learnt to help improve Indian enterprises, as Mr Tata had suggested.

The Boston Consulting Group (BCG), a rapidly rising star in strategy and management consulting, which had a fledgling consulting operation in India then, invited me to join them as the chairman of their India practice. BCG was up against McKinsey, which were the first movers in the Indian market when it was opened up to foreign businesses in 1991. BCG had a frugal office in an office block in south Mumbai. I had to squeeze myself into a tiny room, with one table and three chairs, one of which had to be moved around whenever the door was opened to come in or go out to the small office pool outside where two dozen busy people were crammed together.

BCG partners were very gracious. They wanted Shama, my wife, to be comfortable when we returned to India. Since our children remained in the US where they were both working after their graduation, they knew she would miss them greatly. They found exactly the apartment she wanted in Mumbai that looked on to the gorgeous sunsets on the Arabian Sea. She would not have any trouble shifting home, they assured her. When the container with our furniture and appliances landed in Mumbai from the US, a gentleman was deputed to help us.

He met us in the Taj Mahal Hotel where we were staying temporarily. He handed me his visiting card as he introduced himself. It had his name and beneath his name it stated his profession—'Consultant'.

'I am a consultant too! What consulting do you do?' I asked him.

'I make sure people coming to India from abroad are able to settle into their new homes without any trouble. I ask them what they need and find solutions for them,' he explained. 'They may have brought appliances that run on 120 V and need them to run on 240 V in India. They may need domestic helpers who speak English. Or, they may want their damaged furniture repaired. Whatever it is, I find the best solutions for them.'

India had changed a lot in the eleven years I was in the US. The economy had been opened up to investments, businesses, and ideas from outside India. Consulting had become a fashionable word; people providing different types of services declared themselves 'consultants'—there was the man finding help for my wife, there were many retired people offering a variety of professional services, there were also hundreds of young people from the Indian institutes of management for whom consulting had become their preferred profession and now, I too had joined the bandwagon.

As a lateral hire in an international consulting company, I learnt a lot about the many identities of consulting and also, what the essence of consulting is. This book is a collection of stories of what I have learnt in my ten remarkable years in the USA, then in another ten after I returned to India in 2000 as a professional consultant and subsequently, as I continued to 'consult' in other ways.

I hope young people, as well as others who are wondering what they might do as consultants, will enjoy these stories.

SHOULD A FOREIGN CONSULTANT
ADVISE A NATIONAL GOVERNMENT?

Consultants often have conflicts of interests. They must be guided by their values; not get swayed by public opinion.

The Indian government's policies are being shaped by foreign consultants, an economist complained recently in one of the innumerable webinars I attended during the Covid-19 lockdown. The webinar was about what the government should do to recover the country's shattered economy. He said foreign consultants are advising the government on every policy: industrial, education, health, technology, financial and even the reorganization of government ministries. These young consultants, many of them fresh out of management schools, are swarming all over government, he observed.

It was not like this in 2004 when I had to even defend the government's invitation to a handful of consultants, including myself, to participate in committees which the Planning Commission had set up for a midterm review of the tenth Five-Year Plan. We were invited to participate in our personal capacities, pro bono of course, as a service to the nation.

In the committee I had to review the condition of India's Micro, Small and Medium Enterprises (MSME) sector and its informal industrial sector. I was happy to serve. When I came out of the conference room in the Planning Commission on the conclusion of the first meeting, I was stunned by flashing cameras and quite literally mobbed by reporters. At first, I thought they were looking for someone behind me and tried to move past them. However, it was me they wanted! Microphones were thrust towards my face. 'Are you going to resign?' they asked.

I was stumped. 'Resign from what?' I asked.

'This committee!' a reporter explained. 'All the other consultants from McKinsey, KPMG and Accenture have already resigned from their committees. You have not.'

'Resigned! Why?' I asked.

'Because the Left parties in the government coalition have made a public statement that the government must not allow foreigners to advise India's national Planning Commission. Will you not resign as the others have?'

I had not been aware of this fast-spreading controversy. I had not heard the breaking news in the morning as I had been locked up in the conference room for three hours with my phone switched off. 'Will you, or won't you? Yes or No?' several reporters asked. They wanted a sound bite.

'I will not,' I said.

'Why not?' they chorused.

'I have been invited by the government to serve the country. I will continue to do so until the government tells me that my services are no longer required. I will not withdraw my services,' I said.

I called Montek Singh Ahluwalia, the deputy chairman of the Planning Commission, as soon as I could. He had invited me and the other consultants to serve on the committees. He explained to me what had happened. The United Progressive Alliance had formed the government in a coalition between the Congress and the Left parties. Whereas Dr Manmohan Singh, the prime minister and chairman of the Planning Commission, and he, as deputy chairman of the commission, were keen to continue with the globalization of the Indian economy, which they had begun with the economic reforms of 1991, the Left parties were wary of the influence of the 'Washington Consensus' on India's policies. To them, the appearance of foreign consultants in advisory groups, all of whom were employed by US-based consulting companies (I was with BCG as chairman of its India practice), appeared like the thin end of a big capitalist wedge.

My candid reply to the reporters earlier that I would not resign unless the government wanted me to, had already been flashed on TV screens as 'breaking news', making me a celebrity for the moment. Montek had already seen the flash. He said the other consultants had been pressed to resign by their partners to avoid any damage to their consultancy's brands. He said he would understand it if I too resigned, though he would like me to continue.

The controversy attracted great attention in the media. Rajdeep Sardesai, the celebrity anchor of the NDTV show *The Big Fight*, asked me to participate in a debate on his show.

He said he would invite some leaders of the Left parties too to the debate. He urged me to accept, as a public discussion of differing points of view would lend clarity to the whole matter of foreign consultants in Indian advisory groups. My partners in BCG were torn. They were concerned about the damage to BCG's brand should the debate go the wrong way. However, they left the matter to my judgement and allowed me to do what I felt was best for the country and for BCG too.

I stepped into the ring. Rajdeep had also persuaded A.B. Bardhan, general secretary of the Communist Party of India, to join in *The Big Fight* along with two economists, one from the famous Left-leaning Jawaharlal Nehru University and the other an economist with a doctorate from a foreign university. There were fifty spectators in the studio looking forward to a good fight, with Rajdeep whipping up their expectations (and his show's television rating points [TRPs]).

Mr Bardhan presented his case eloquently. He said, there are millions of capable Indians who could advise the government, then why did the government need to turn to foreigners? 'This is India's colonial hangover,' he said. 'We look up to people and ideas that come from outside the country, especially the West, and look down upon our own people who know their country better.'

In *The Big Fight* format, there is no time to beat around the bush. One must be direct; so I was. 'Wasn't Karl Marx a foreigner?' I asked Mr Bardhan. 'Why then does your party continue to quote him and spread his ideas in India?' I challenged him.

'One should take the best ideas from wherever one can so long as they serve the people of India,' Mr Bardhan defended himself. 'However, the people who bring the ideas to India must be loyal to India and not serve foreign masters,' he quipped.

'Are you doubting my loyalty to my country?' I asked.

He fumbled and then recovered. 'No. I am not. But you have to serve your foreign masters too who pay you. You have to support their ideology.'

'I was invited to advise the Planning Commission in my personal capacity, and as an Indian, and not as an employee or representative of a foreign consultancy,' I countered.

'It is hard to discriminate what is good for India unless you really know India and what is good for the country,' he responded.

'I have spent almost my whole life in India. I care for my country and my people. Who is to judge who cares more or less? I cannot judge whether you care more than I do.'

Mr Bardhan was very gracious. 'I am not doubting you personally, Mr Maira,' he said. 'But I do worry when people look down on us and push down their ideas on us claiming they must be better because they are from abroad.'

I agreed with him on that point.

Rajdeep Sardesai ended the debate with a poll. The question was, 'Should the Government of India have invited consultants with foreign experience to advise it?' The results were a resounding—Yes.

After the public debate, Montek Singh Ahluwalia called me to thank me on behalf of the prime minister and himself.

A few days later, he informed me that the government was closing down the consultative committees because of the political controversy. Therefore, I did not have to resign. However, I could not be on the government advisory committees either.

Five years later, when Dr Manmohan Singh became prime minister for the second time, I was invited by him to become a full-fledged member of the Planning Commission, which he chaired, to advise the country on a policy for industry. Dr Manmohan Singh had led the Congress Party to an electoral victory after standing up to the Left parties that had objected to his signing the nuclear energy pact with the USA. The Congress did not need their support any longer to form a government.

Just a few months earlier I had already hung up my boots as the chairman of BCG. So in July 2009, when Dr Manmohan Singh administered to me the oath to serve India and its Constitution, along with the other members of the Planning Commission, I became an official consultant to the Government of India.

COACHES, CONSULTANTS, FACILITATORS AND LEADERS

A great leader of people is a coach to the people; not their boss.

A coach does not play the game himself. He enables players to play the game well to win. Great coaches give advice to players on strategies. They also guide players on how to improve their physical as well as mental capabilities.

Consultants have many profiles; like coaches, they too assist their clients in a variety of ways. Some guide their clients with strategies to win, others help their clients to build their organization's capabilities. Some consultants do both—guide the client with strategy as well as help the client to build the muscles necessary to execute the strategy. Such consultants can be great coaches.

On the other hand, there is a vast majority of consultants who fix things for their clients such as a broken process like a plumber who fixes a leak, or tidy up things for their clients like an interior decorator who improves the layout of a room. And, some consultants are like 'special tools' which a client can hire for a task they need to get done for which it is not worthwhile to have a permanent capacity in-house. Increasing demand for consultants, who do not merely advise but 'implement' their advice too, has boosted the growth of consulting companies. Consulting companies need large teams of people to go in and tidy up things for their clients. Most consultants in such implementation teams must think less and do more, whereas good consultant-coaches 'implement' very little themselves because the players they coach must 'do it' on the field.

Innovation Associates (IA) was a tiny consulting company in the 1990s. It employed less than fifty people—including the secretaries in the office who managed the travel and preparation of presentations for the consultants who were always somewhere else coaching and training their clients. The firm, founded by Charlie Kieffer and Peter Senge, both physicists from Massachusetts Institute of Technology (MIT), took off when Senge's book, *The Fifth Discipline: The Art and Practice of the Learning Organization* (1990) became a bestseller.

Senge's thesis was that organizations and their leaders must learn and improve their capabilities if they want to fulfil the purposes for which the organizations are created, especially when the world around them is changing constantly. Organizations must master 'five disciplines', he said. One, their leaders must have 'personal mastery'; two, they must become aware of their own 'mental models' which they may have to change as the world changes; three, they must have capabilities to create a 'shared vision'; and four, they must promote 'team learning'. The fifth discipline which leaders and their teams must master, he urged, was 'systems thinking'.

Peter Senge, Charlie Kieffer and other IA consultants designed and delivered packaged training programmes for each of the disciplines to teach executives how to apply these disciplines in their work and in their personal lives too. These programmes constituted IA's intellectual property. Companies paid large amounts of money for their executives to attend the short 'public' programmes in which thirty or so executives from various companies participated. The training programmes fetched good business for the consultants. Once the programme had been designed, the delivery cost was small. The only recurring expenditure was the cost of time of the two IA consultants who conducted each programme, and overheads for the facility where the training was delivered.

IA had two wings: the 'training' wing which delivered the training programmes, and a 'consulting' wing. While the training wing delivered the public programmes to executives from various companies together, the consulting wing assisted a company to apply the disciplines internally. IA's consulting wing would make an assessment of a company's specific needs and customize a suite of internal training programmes for it.

The consulting wing had a flagship product, the Visionary Leadership and Planning (VLP) programme. In this programme, the training in the five disciplines was delivered to company executives while they were developing the vision for their company, and then scanning the world around their company using systems thinking. Disciplines of personal mastery and mental models were custom-made appropriately and delivered as needed. The executives worked in tandem and were coached to improve their own team's learning.

VLP was a profitable consulting product. Generally, one or two consultants were required to assist the client and that too sporadically. The consultants were not expected to have much domain knowledge, if at all, of the client's business. Rather, they were expected to be masters at developing the client organization's ability to learn for itself—to become 'a learning organization'. Therefore, IA did not have to depute teams of young consultants to do any research or number crunching. The clients were expected to handle this with their internal resources preferably or, if necessary, hire another consultant with domain knowledge.

NASA's aeronautical division, which was going through hard times in the 1990s with the cutbacks in public grants for its programmes, had hired ADL to design a strategy to commercialize NASA's cutting-edge technologies. The division had also hired IA's consulting wing to apply the VLP process to assist NASA leaders and teams to navigate tough internal changes. Thus, while ADL was guiding NASA with the 'technical' side of its strategy, IA was assisting with its 'social' side. The head of the NASA division felt that the two sides fitted splendidly with each other and he stated that it would be much easier for him and his team if the two consulting organizations would work as one team combining their competencies into one seamless process. Spurred by the need of their common client, the two consulting teams set aside two days to look into each other's processes and discern the possibility of developing a combined process.

Officially, I was in the ADL team since I was employed by ADL. However, I had already attended some IA training programmes to learn the methods of personal mastery and systems thinking which I felt would be valuable for the human-centred manufacturing management practice I was leading in ADL. Moreover, Charlie Kieffer and Peter Senge felt I was aligned with their way of thinking and consulting as they had read my book, *The Accelerating Organization: Embracing the Human Face of Change,* in which I had described a method for facilitating the creation of a high-performing 'learning organization' based on my experience with Cemex, the Mexican cement company (which I have described in the story 'Speaking the Same Language') and other consulting projects. Thus, I had my foot in both camps and was able to unite minds when they seemed to fall apart.

The ADL-IA meeting wasn't an easy one. If NASA hadn't forced the two to work together, they might have continued to spar within NASA to prove which of them was more deserving—experts with deep domain knowledge, which the ADL consultants preferred to call themselves, or mere 'facilitators', which the ADL consultants pejoratively referred to the IA consultants as. However, they did develop a way of working together as one team for NASA.

The head of the NASA division said his colleagues and he had worked with a number of consultants over the years. Some were outstanding in their knowledge of their industry and technology, like ADL, while others were very good with organization behaviour and change management, like IA. He said the combined process for NASA, which the two teams had developed together, was the most effective consulting intervention he had ever experienced.

Following this success, leaders of ADL and IA decided to merge the two companies to offer their integrated consulting services around the world through ADL's global network. This service was not pure 'consulting', in the form of providing strategic solutions, nor was it pure 'facilitation'. It was a combination of both. It was 'consultative facilitation', which is the method applied by great coaches who know the strategies of the game very well and who also know how to strengthen their players' will to win.

I have often reflected on what great leaders do. What was Sumant Moolgaokar's leadership method? Moolgaokar was chairman of The Tata Engineering and Locomotive Company (TELCO)—which was later renamed Tata Motors. I was privileged to serve with him for twenty years. He has been acknowledged in India as an industrial leader par excellence. His 'domain knowledge' of the commercial vehicle industry and its technologies was as good as anybody's in the world. He was, undoubtedly, the 'big boss' for everyone.

Moolgaokar's mission was to build a 'learning factory'— an organization that learnt to accomplish through the years what it could not at its inception. Moreover, it had to learn faster than any other organization in the same industry across the world, he insisted. The principles of VLP, as well as the disciplines of systems thinking and team learning, came to him instinctively and he applied them remarkably, though he had not been to any training programmes in those disciplines.

Moolgaokar was a great coach to many people around him. He made them aspire for greater achievements. He would observe them at play in the organization, reflect with them on their progress, and guide them towards what they should learn in order to improve. His mastery of the art of consultative facilitation made him a great leader of people.

WHEN THE JOB IS DONE

Consultants cannot count how well they have served a client by counting the amount of money the client continues to pay for the service.

Two speakers stepped up to their podiums, 10 metres apart, to tell us their story—a remarkable story that involved both of them. In the audience we were 100 members of the Society of Organizational Learning. One of the speakers was a senior executive of British Petroleum (BP) and the other was Richard Pascale, a widely admired teacher and consultant who had guided BP's leadership team through a remarkable turnaround. The audience had come to listen to him and to learn the story of the BP turnaround.

Richard Pascale was respected in business circles as a great turnaround consultant. He had worked early on as a consultant with McKinsey. A respected professor at Stanford Business School for twenty years and currently an associate fellow of the Säid Business School at the University of Oxford, Pascale is a well-known author too. His book *Managing on the Edge* (1990) is a bestseller as was his earlier book *The Art of Japanese Management* (1981) which he co-authored with Anthony Athos.

Pascale chose to tell the story in an unusual way—as an interaction between a client and a consultant. The conversation began with the stage lights on BP's executive. He recounted the discussions within the BP team when they realized that the company was in trouble. They knew they needed help. They met with many consultants who were keen to help—for a substantial fee of course—and they even engaged some to help BP improve parts of its operations. However, what John Brown, the CEO of BP, was looking for was a consultant who could help the leadership team improve its own competency to lead. BP researched and requested Pascale to meet the team in London, if he was willing.

The spotlight shifted to Pascale, who recounted what was on his mind when he had received BP's request. He had worked with many CEOs and their teams before. They all seemed to enjoy the scheduled meetings, and he was paid well too, but not much changed in the companies' operations following the meetings. Pascale had enjoyed the preliminary meeting with BP's team. They exuded an energy that excited him. They were also very direct with him as they sized him up. He, on the other hand, was curious about what was going on in their minds.

The spotlight shifted back to the BP executive on the other side of the room and we heard what went on in the minds of the team members as they assessed their prospective consultant. They had spent a lot of money previously for the services of globally acclaimed consulting companies, but to no avail. Now they were looking for a consultant with a difference. Though they were not sure at this point, Pascale did seem different.

The spotlight moved back to Pascale who described the contract made between him and the team. They would begin working together, but if any side was not satisfied, they could walk away.

The spotlight went back and forth a few times as the two speakers wove their stories together. The company was turning around well. Pascale was flying into BP's meetings frequently. The chemistry between the client and the consultant was working very well. A strategy was adopted. It was being implemented. Signs of success were beginning to appear.

Then the spotlight went off for a brief while and the audience heard Pascale's voice coming from the shadows. When the lights came back on him, we saw a sad-looking man whose energy had gone out of him. Pascale said the meetings with BP had become less frequent. Pascale was a professor in Stanford in California. One day he learnt from a friend that BP's executive team was meeting in California. He could have easily attended that meeting. Why was he not invited? Was this a signal of his failure to live up to BP's expectations? He called the team leader who immediately invited him for dinner with them.

Pascale said he was surprised by the bonhomie with which he was received when he came into the room. The team seemed to have had a good day together and were happy to see him too. They were not avoiding him. However, he felt neglected so he ventured to ask whether his services were no longer useful. When he asked, he was met with a surprised silence.

He recalled his feelings of confusion and hurt. The spotlight remained on him. Then another spotlight came on the BP executive. He turned from the audience and looked calmly into Pascale's face across the room and spoke to him.

Wasn't it the consultant's aim to help the team to learn to work effectively together, find its own strategies and start implementing them? Isn't that what they had asked his help for and what he had clearly said was all he wanted to do? In fact, they had selected him over other consultants who had offered to provide many other services for the company. But BP had not wanted that. It wanted to be self-reliant. Why then was Pascale unhappy to find the BP team looking confident and not needing to lean on him any longer?

Having posed these penetrating questions to Pascale, the client stepped off the stage.

Pascale then turned to his audience, who were mostly consultants in organizational learning. He asked them to reflect for a moment why they had chosen to become consultants. The gist of their responses was that they wanted to help their clients to become more confident and more capable of achieving their goals.

'What is the mission of a medical doctor?' he asked.

'To make their patients healthy,' the audience responded.

'Isn't your mission the same?' he asked. 'If your client is unwell, you must restore them back to health. Isn't your job done then? Haven't you fulfilled your responsibility when your client feels confident that they do not need you any longer?'

During those days, I was learning to become a successful consultant in ADL. However, the company was going through an existential crisis at that time. Though it was the world's oldest consulting company, its growth was stagnating. The other management consulting companies that had spawned from ADL—the Boston Consulting Group and Bain & Company—were already growing much faster than ADL. They were chasing the venerable McKinsey & Company—a clear leader in management consulting at that time. Moreover, younger partners in all these companies were far richer than ADL's more seasoned consultants. An analysis of the operational models of the most successful companies by ADL revealed that their partners were rewarded for building long, multi-year client relationships and for obtaining repeat business from the same clients.

The ethics of the medical profession can provide an insightful analogy for this version of consulting. Is the best doctor one to whom the patient must keep returning and paying? Or, is that doctor the best to whom the patient pays the least for becoming healthy sooner? Patients feel the inconvenience of paying too much for their healthcare. This is because doctors are rewarded by hospitals for prescribing more tests and also for referring patients to other doctors. Such practices increase the incomes of doctors and the profits of hospitals. Patients might benefit too but they have to pay a heavy price, much more than they need to.

So, the million-dollar question is: Shouldn't a competent and ethical doctor be delighted when his patient does not need him any longer and therefore does not call?

'What should be the ethics of a good consultant then?' asked Pascale.

WHEN CONSULTING
BECOMES A BUSINESS

When consultants measure their success by the amount of money they earn and the success of their company by its size, they risk losing sight of the purpose of their profession.

Quite recently, a senior professional in London, who was exploring a career transition to management consulting, passed on to me a story in the *New York Times*. He was studying for an executive MBA and was planning to join a consulting company, but on reading the story, he said he had changed his mind.

The story, *As McKinsey Sells Advice, Its Hedge Fund May Have a Stake in the Outcome,* was published in February 2019. It is a troubling account of the conflicts of interest of well-paid consultants who advise firms on their business strategies while, at the same time, they make investments in various forms in financial enterprises to multiply their own wealth. Though the story is about the iconic McKinsey & Company that was founded in 1926, it is a scathing comment on the management consulting industry as a whole, and also raises pertinent questions about the ethics of business enterprises.

The foundations of the management consulting business were laid by venerable men, like Marvin Bower of McKinsey and Bruce Henderson of BCG. They had enjoined their consulting companies' partners to be trusted advisers to CEOs and offer them objective advice to improve the performance of their businesses. Their predecessor was Dr Arthur Dehon Little of MIT, who had created a consulting company in 1886, Arthur D. Little Inc. (ADL), to assist businessmen to turn scientific ideas into commercial products to serve society's needs and make business profits. Other consulting firms such as the immensely successful BCG (1963) and Bain & Company (1973) not only emerged from ADL but also flourished substantially. Management consulting became a very respectable profession and business school graduates, selected by the leading strategy firms, received the highest salaries—especially those in McKinsey.

I worked with ADL in the USA from 1989 to 1999. Those were the heady days of capitalist enterprises. Socialism, or at least communism, was supposedly dead with the fall of the Soviet Union. Stock markets rose. New computation technologies powered the dot.com boom. Young people were becoming millionaires overnight without spending years slogging as consultants.

An existential challenge

For some of the 'best of the best' management consultants working with McKinsey, Bain and other firms, there arose an existential challenge: If they were so smart, why did it not reflect in their earnings? Some of them left their companies to start their own ventures, and succeeded. Since smart people are the only resources of any management consulting company, the firms had to come up with ways to retain them. A transformation took place in consulting companies—from being trusted advisers to their clients, they turned into creative enterprises that would enable their partners to partake in the gravy of the capitalist boom.

The heady changes in the consulting industry also affected ADL in its quiet campus in Acorn Park, in Cambridge, Massachusetts, where its consultants were exploring new technologies and management solutions for their clients. ADL could not offer the new business graduates the same financial rewards that the other companies were offering. Moreover, it had a different business model. Whereas the others sought to make their clients dependent on them, building long relationships from which they could draw large streams of fees, the ADL philosophy was to do the job and leave until invited to return—no hanging around. However, it wasn't a financially lucrative strategy for the consulting firm. So, ADL began to rethink its consulting strategy to emulate the extended-engagement model, at which McKinsey was the best.

But even this model was not sufficient to produce the new wealth McKinsey's partners wanted to earn to keep up with the wealth of young entrepreneurs who started their own businesses. So, as the *New York Times* reported, McKinsey's partners began to explore other avenues which, as one road leads to another, seem to have brought them twenty years later to Guernsey Island and other tax havens and into law courts to defend their integrity. They had created new investment vehicles for the consulting company's partners to invest in business ventures. New entities were formed in which consultants could invest their sweat equity along with their money. Thus, webs of ventures grew within which the financial interests of consultants became tangled with their professional ethics. McKinsey was not able to convince the courts that the 'ethical screen' between these ventures was strong enough to keep the consultants focused solely on their roles as trusted advisers to their clients, the purpose for which their eminent founder had created the firm. McKinsey maintained that there was no wrongdoing.

The partners of management consulting companies were confronted with ethical dilemmas while adapting to the paradigm that the 'purpose of a business is to increase shareholder value', and with it, the culture of 'more wealth is better' (and even 'greed is good') that had begun to spread across the capitalist world since the 1990s. When the partners of BCG met to approve a proposition to create a vehicle for them to invest in technology start-ups, a young partner stood up and asked all partners to rethink why they had joined the firm. He spoke for himself saying he had been inspired by the call to be a 'trusted adviser' who would help business leaders to do the right things and do them well. If the clients valued our advice they would pay for it and that was the ethical way to make money, he said. We must not get diverted from the mission in order to pursue more wealth for ourselves, he urged.

The debate within ADL was more divisive. The firm had many wise old-timers who had spent their lives revelling in the intellectual challenges imposed by their clients. Their satisfaction was in finding innovative technical and managerial solutions and in helping their clients to apply those solutions. NASA was among ADL's largest clients. ADL's environmental practice was one of its most successful ones in the 1990s, long before the threat of climate change compelled businesses to pay more attention to their impact on the environment. However, the new ADL partners, many of them 'laterals' from other consulting companies, were impatient with such values-based practices. They wanted to earn more money. ADL had troves of intellectual property which they wanted to monetize and produce more wealth for the partners. They made innovative new deals with investors to carve out their monetary value. This conflict between heightened pursuit of money and entrenched ethical values of the consultants caused a 100-year-old firm to implode.

'You have to decide, am I a consulting firm or an investment firm?' the *New York Times* article quoted Charles Elson, a finance professor at the University of Delaware who focuses on corporate governance. 'They're two different things,' Elson says.

Faulty measures of success

A doctor is expected to be a trusted adviser with only the patient's interest in mind. But a doctor who encourages the patient to use more investigative and therapeutic services, only to increase the revenue flow from the client, is not working in the client's best interests even if the services provide some marginal value to the client. If the doctor has a financial stake in the provision of these services, this can even be considered an unethical practice.

Whenever doctors and hospitals become 'businesses' such ethical issues will arise. It is the same for the media too, which is expected to work in the public interest. The ethical question for all professionals is, what is the purpose of the service they provide to their clients and to society? Is it to produce more returns for themselves, or to improve their clients' and society's well-being? The simple answer is—both.

But life is never so simple. When the pursuit of wealth takes over, the original purpose of the enterprise is compromised. When the principal measure of success of an enterprise depends on its revenue influx and the wealth earned by its investors (or, in the case of a consulting business, its partners), society loses something. It loses professionals with integrity; it loses enterprises that can be trusted to maximize their clients' gains. The timbre of institutions that society looks up to cracks.

The technology industry is going through a big existential crisis for this very reason. It was much admired for the exciting new innovations it had created—social media that enabled people to reach out, search engines that assisted people to find any information they wanted, and apps for instant gratification. Their owners have become some of the richest persons in the world. Initially, these enterprises were seen, naively, as God's gifts to mankind, but within a few years their dark sides have been exposed. The purpose of these enterprises was never to provide a public service. It was to create more wealth for their owners.

Management schools teach people how to get things done efficiently. There is very little introspection about the social purposes for which these acquired skills should be used. In fact, what business schools have been teaching is that the principal measure of success of a business is how much value it can create for its shareholders by efficiently extracting the environmental and societal resources it uses. The success of a business is not gauged by the positive impact it has on the lives of people and on the environment but ranked by its shareholders' wealth and its revenues. These are self-referential, even selfish, measures of success.

Even large, not-for-profit organizations in the social sector use such self-referential measures to determine how effective they are. Their boards examine the growth of the budgets of their organizations and set goals to double or even triple their own sizes, presuming that if they expand the world will benefit. Rarely do the boards spend time to reflect on the value their organizations actually provide to society, or find innovative ways to increase their beneficial impact while remaining small themselves. Catalysts of improvement in the world around them—social-sector organizations and trusted advisers—do not have to be large themselves. They must learn to induce improvement in the world with minimal increase in their own size.

When the budgets of organizations become large, it is only a small step to justify larger salaries for managers. The salaries of CEOs are often a substantial percentage of the budget. So, while organizations justify higher salaries, they lose sight of the purpose of the enterprise. One of India's largest and most admired trusts lost its tax exemption because its CEO was earning about $3,00,000 per annum. The charity commissioners felt such a high salary, which a large, profitable business could have justified perhaps, was not in line with the charitable purpose of the organization.

There is nothing evil about wanting to be wealthy. The question is, how wealthy does one need to be? If the answer is, to be as wealthy as others, which is what seems to be driving the behaviours of many professionals, doctors and consultants, the race is on, in an upward spiral, in which the wealthy look for ways to become even wealthier. Somewhere along the way, they lose sight of the original purpose of the enterprise and also lose their ethical moorings.

These days business schools are rated by the salaries their graduates are offered by employers who compete with each other to hire from the best-rated schools. The best schools attract the best students. Thus, in a reinforcing cycle, money becomes the measure of success for students. The 'best of the best' are tempted to join professional firms driven by the salary they are offered. In such cultures, principles of service, societal trust and ethics become hard to learn and hard to teach.

I find many people today wanting to opt out of this money culture, like the senior professional in London who has changed his mind about joining a consulting firm. Many business schools are searching for ways for their students to acquire an ethical orientation, and some consulting companies are trying to return to their ethical moorings. The social and business culture of greed for more wealth, in which they are all trapped, will not be easy to change. But it must be changed to make the world better for everyone.

The established order will resist changes that leaders of change want to bring about. Thomas Kuhn's classic, *The Structure of Scientific Revolutions,* explained why those who are aligned with the prevalent paradigm of ideas, and are powerful in institutions founded on those ideas, will feel threatened by any new idea. They will fight back.

The powerful global empire of financial investors and shareholders will strike back at uppity business leaders who break out of the paradigm. Paul Polman, CEO of Unilever for ten years—St Paul as he was called, reverentially by some, and sarcastically by others—was brought down by a backlash from shareholders. They felt that he was going too far in meeting the needs of other stakeholders.

Consultants advocating for more 'corporate social responsibility' (CSR) are expected to establish the 'business case' for it. They must prove to business leaders that CSR will produce more returns for shareholders in the long run. Otherwise, it does not hold water. This is the selfish, self-referential paradigm of business responsibility that must be changed. It is a struggle between the empire and the people and the Earth. Now, the Earth and the people are rumbling, contesting the power of the global financial empire.

Leaders of change will be those who will take the first step towards shaping a better world for everyone, regardless of whether others will follow them or not. They will look inwards to rediscover the purpose of their existence and reset their own measures of success. They will not be waiting for others to change first, for then they will not be leaders.

(This story was published on the website of Founding Fuel in 2020.)

EARNING RESPECT

Workers want respect from their managers, their fellow citizens and from consultants too.

Elections for the mayor of Mexico City were coming up. The incumbent mayor wanted to win of course. However, citizens were not satisfied with his performance. The quality of municipal services was not commensurate with the taxes and service fees they paid. They complained that the municipality's payrolls were bloated with salaries of staff who did not serve them well. An opposition candidate said he would improve the services if he was elected. The writing was on the wall. Unless services improved rapidly before the elections, the incumbent mayor would lose.

He commissioned two management consulting companies to assist. One was ADL, where I was working. ADL's Mexican consultants had recently concluded a successful engagement with Cemex, the Mexican cement company, to rapidly improve the performance of its cement plants. It had deployed a bottom-up approach, with an effective methodology for engaging the workers to make improvements. They proposed to use this tactic to improve the city services. The mayor was intrigued by it but did not want to take any risk, so he hired another company also.

The other consulting company had a large practice for improving government services using the conventional approach of 'process re-engineering'. It provided its credentials to the mayor, and he was impressed. Mexico City is one of the largest cities in the world with a population of 22 million (in 2020). The mayor assigned a greater part of the city to this company to make improvements on and only a small part to ADL.

The ADL consultants began their assignment in earnest, as they had at Cemex, by engaging all employees as well as their managers to understand their individual aspirations and find out their views on what changes were required. The managers complained about the lack of funds to improve the infrastructure and lazy, uncooperative workers.

When the workers were asked what they aspired for most in their lives, they said it was 'respect'. They not only wanted respect from their managers but also, surprisingly, what mattered most to them was to get respect from the citizens of Mexico City. They felt that, like their managers, their neighbours too did not respect them and thought that municipal workers were overpaid and generally lazy. Some even said their children were reluctant to admit in school, whenever a discussion came up about the poor services in the city, that their fathers were municipal workers.

The ADL consultants asked the workers to think about why the citizens did not respect them and what needed to be changed to earn back their respect. They were encouraged to list the requirements in two categories—the actions required by management and others, and the actions they could take themselves. ADL helped them to sort out these prerequisites in terms of impact they would have—to get them citizens' respect and the feasibility of taking the actions quickly—in terms of the costs involved and management approvals necessary.

The citizens were complaining about the tardiness and surliness of services. Precisely the reason why managers too blamed the workers as the root cause of the municipality's poor performance. In this, the managers and citizens seemed to be aligned.

A deep introspection revealed that the reason for workers' stubbornly resisting to improve their services was because they disliked their managers and did not want to cooperate with them, and not because they did not like the citizens they served. Often, the citizens would be angry and rude to them and that offended the workers. However, they did admit that the citizens' complaints against them were justified.

Some groups amongst the workers decided to conduct an experiment to see if they could earn the respect of the citizens by changing their own behaviour. The operators of the toll booths in the area did a quick survey, on their own, and asked the citizens what improvement they could bring about in their services. The changed attitude of the toll booth workers pleasantly surprised the citizens and this began to change the citizens' attitudes towards them. The workers analysed what needed improvement urgently and asked ADL to arrange for quick training for them, as well as help them to make small changes in their workplaces to enable them to provide services more efficiently.

The managers were unfamiliar with this positive side of the workers. They too, cautiously, changed their attitude towards them and decided to cooperate. The toll booth manager expedited procurement of new uniforms for the workers which they had been demanding for some time. The citizens were very happy to see noticeable changes in toll booth services within a few weeks.

The workers carried out another survey and made further changes. The citizens noticed that too and were beginning to talk to the workers with new-found respect. Observing the success of the experiment in the toll booths, other sections of workers followed their example. A bottom-up process began scaling up.

The mayor called for a midterm review of the progress of the projects with both consultants. The consultants of the other company, dressed in their sharp dark suits and ties, made an impressive PowerPoint presentation. The ADL report was presented by well-dressed presenters, who had some slides too, albeit simpler ones. In their slides they reported the surveys of citizens' expectations as well as confirmations from the citizens of the improvements that were made. They also presented some 'before and after' photographs of the places where services had been revamped, such as the toll booths and the licence registry.

The mayor was clearly impressed. He thought the presenters were ADL consultants. He asked the ADL partner sitting beside him how they had been able to motivate the workers so quickly. The partner said, 'Why don't you ask the workers themselves. They are in front of you, telling you their story themselves!'

ADL had invested some of its consulting fees to buy suits and ties for the workers and had helped them prepare their presentations. The mayor jested that the workers could become ADL consultants and assist with the changes in other parts of the city.

Unfortunately, the mayor did not get re-elected and the overall change in the city was too insignificant to be noteworthy. However, Douglas McGregor's 'Theory Y' had been proved once again, that workers are intrinsically motivated and enjoy the challenge of work for their own self-respect. Yet, 'Theory X', that workers are intrinsically lazy and are shirkers, and therefore need 'sticks and carrots' to drive them, remains a widespread theory-in-use for managing workers.

WHAT MONEY CAN'T BUY

Many young people today want to measure the worthiness of their lives not by how much money they earn but by the improvement they can make to the conditions of the environment and society.

I have used the image of the Petronas Twin Towers in Kuala Lumpur in the Preface to describe the connections between the worlds of business, management education and management consulting.

The Petronas Twin Towers in Kuala Lumpur, the tallest twin towers in the world, are connected by a double-decker skybridge 170 metres above ground, which is the highest two-storey bridge in the world. It enables people at the uppermost levels of the towers to cross over without bothering to come down to the ground at all.

In the world of wealth, one tower is the education tower with business schools on top. The other is the corporate tower with C-suites of the largest multinational firms at its apex. The best students from the best schools in business are picked by marquee international consulting companies, such as McKinsey & Company, Boston Consulting Group, and Bain & Company. They cross the skybridge to advise CEOs and CXOs in offices at the top of the other tower. Business schools provide a fast elevator for students who want to earn high salaries quickly. Many join management consulting companies. Management consulting provides a bridge between the world of education and the world of business, high up in the sky.

In the new millennium many young persons, who have reached the top of the education tower by the fast elevator through management schools, are looking for another bridge to connect with the world. They are not inclined to work in the world of business.

In 2006, before the global financial crisis, when the Dow Jones was reaching heights it had never reached before, an important meeting was convened in Cleveland. The subject of the meeting was 'Business as an Agent of World Benefit'. The provocation for the meeting was the increasing evidence from several multi-country surveys of the declining trust in business corporations. Evidently, as consumers, people seemed satisfied with the products and services provided by corporations, and as investors delighted by their stocks' performance, but as citizens they expected much more from corporations.

The meeting was convened by the Academy of Management and the UN Global Compact. The Academy of Management is the largest organization of business management teachers in the world with more than 18,000 members. As one of its members said, it is the 'Teamsters

Union' of business teachers. The UN Global Compact, founded in 2000, is an international organization of business corporations that volunteered to conduct their businesses in ways that would accelerate achievement of the Millennium Development Goals. Beginning with forty members in 2000, the compact had more than 3000 members in six continents by 2006.

The backdrop of the meeting was the conditions of people and the environment, neither of which seemed to be improving as rapidly as was required to achieve the Millennium Development Goals. Meanwhile, businesses were reporting sterling financial performance. Therefore, a lurking suspicion (contributing to the widespread mistrust of business corporations) was that not only are the philanthropic and CSR undertakings of the corporations inadequate, but that the core operations of businesses may be, somehow, contributing to the unsatisfactory conditions of people and the environment.

The meeting was attended by 450 persons from forty countries—management students, business school teachers, administrators and corporate executives—and another 1000 people attended via webcast. Over three days, several thought leaders in the corporate and education worlds discussed more than a hundred papers and carried on a lively dialogue facilitated by David Cooperrider of Case Western University, using the principles of 'appreciative inquiry' that he had developed, whereby the intelligence of many participants can be combined in large meetings.

The views of the students were revealing. A survey of 2100 students in eighty-seven business schools found that 87 per cent of them believed that corporations should work towards broader societal goals, but only 18 per cent believed they were actually doing so. While 36 per cent felt business schools were preparing business managers to work for the betterment of society, 70 per cent wanted business schools to change their curriculum to develop socially and environmentally responsible individuals, and 79 per cent said they wanted socially responsible jobs. What is also revealing is that while 63 per cent of the respondents said they would work for a medium and large company after graduation, only 33 per cent said they would continue to work there after five to ten years. The reason was since they had to repay the loans they had taken for their education, they needed the salaries the big companies paid, but after repaying the loans they would rather do more socially responsible work.

The young teacher who presented the survey had selected two statements she thought expressed the students' feelings overall. One was: 'The key business role is to develop society, not profits.' The other: 'Profitability is easy; changing the world is hard.'

A system run by money

Businesses, business schools and management students are part of a system, with each responding to the other. All propose to bring about a change in the system so that business can play a more effective role as an 'agent for world benefit'. But the question is where will the change begin that will change the system?

While discussing what can make corporations work for the greater good of society, the CEOs inferred that if the customers were to demand that companies act responsibly, and if they were to buy their products and services only from those that did, businesses would change their strategies quickly. In other words, these CEOs are calling on customers to take the lead and pressurize business managers to change. They are saying that when people start acting like responsible citizens rather than passive consumers, they can make the companies behave responsibly too.

Business graduates who want to step away from the skybridge leading to the world of business as usual want to act like responsible citizens of society and not merely as wealth creators and consumers. Business schools should change to support them.

The CEOs, educators and students participating in the Cleveland conference discussed the need to change the curriculum of management education. According to the CEOs, graduates produced by the management schools had too narrow a view of the world. They were driven solely by the profit motive, in their own lives and in their view of business's role in society.

The CEOs recommended that the management curriculum should be modified to include compulsory courses on the human condition and the environment, and that the excessive emphasis on economics and finance should be reduced. Endorsing the need for a course correction, a respected American CEO went so far as to say that economics should be removed altogether because its fundamental assumptions about human behaviour were flawed and, instead, the students should be taught to discover and relate to their conscience and learn the art of building human relationships!

A few years ago, recognizing the needs of students who want to serve society and not business, some Indian entrepreneurs took the risky step of creating a management school with a difference—a school for 'development' managers, not business managers. They designed a curriculum for young people who wanted to work as social change-makers. The school's pedagogy was designed for reflective learning blended with experiential learning.

The curriculum of the school seemed to be working well. The end-of-programme evaluations of students, teachers and the course designers, which I participated in, revealed the maturation of the students as well as their appreciation of the reflective and experiential pedagogy. Subsequently, many students had joined social change enterprises or started their own even before their graduation.

The investors of the school decided to scale up the programme and double the numbers of students. For this, they would not only have to attract more students to join but also help a larger number of graduates to find good jobs. They benchmarked the school with other management schools to compete for students and placements. They decided to include conventional 'management' subjects—finance, marketing and operations—to cater to a larger numbers of students. Since the curriculum would have to be crammed into the one-year-long programme, the time allotted for innovative experiential and reflective courses had to be reduced. The curriculum changed from an 80:20 development to management ratio to a 50:50 ratio. Thus, by emulating the practices of the business world, which their students aspired to change in the first place, they came close to a conventional management school.

The educators in the Cleveland meeting retorted that businesses get what they pay for, so business schools get more students in the financial disciplines as they get the highest salaries. Therefore, in the spirit of putting one's money where one's mouth is, if businesses were to pay more to graduates in other disciplines, students would want to take those courses, and the schools would offer them too! However, the educators were in a bind. They admitted that the curriculum was too limited. They cited a study by Jeffrey Pfeffer of Stanford which showed that, whereas students in other educational programmes broaden their thinking, the MBA curriculum produced graduates who were more constricted in their thinking when they left than when they entered the programme. Another contention was that business schools are rated by the salaries their students are offered on graduation, and since students in the financial disciplines get the highest salaries, schools must produce more of them to improve their ratings.

Young people today are searching for meaning in their lives. They want to make the world better, and not just make more money. Some are even turning to philosophers for guidance. Michael Sandel is the Anne T. and Robert M. Bass professor of government theory at Harvard University Law School. His lectures on Philosophy 101 became so popular after the financial crisis that they were moved to the Sanders

Theatre in Cambridge (Mass), which has a seating capacity of 1166. Even this was not enough. His course, Justice, was the university's first course to be made freely available online and on television. Sandel's book *What Money Can't Buy: The Moral Limits of Markets* has become a bestseller—which is remarkable for a book on philosophy!

Sandel explains how, in recent decades, we have drifted from having a market economy to being a market society. Money values have crowded out other norms in almost every aspect of life.

Money plays many roles in our lives. It is a currency to facilitate economic transactions. It provides a common language for buyers and sellers of commodities, whether minerals or music. Money is also a store of economic wealth. It can also be a marker of worthiness of individuals and institutions: those who are affluent are given higher status in market societies. Companies are graded by their monetary valuations on the stock market; countries by the sizes of their gross domestic products (GDPs). Correspondingly, business schools are ranked by how much money their graduates earn.

However, money is not everything. All citizens have equal voting rights in a good democracy, whether they are billionaires or paupers. The students who spoke at the Cleveland meeting and the graduates of the development school in India want to change the way the world works. They do not want to judge the worthiness of their lives by how much money they earn, but by how much good they do.

Businesses, management schools and students are parts of a complex system. Donella H. Meadows, a doyenne of systems thinking, and the author of the report, *The Limits to Growth,* which pointed out in 1972 that the pattern of economic growth the world was following would lead to an environmental crisis, provided the insight that *every system is perfectly designed to produce the results it is presently producing.* All components of the system, responding to each other, are locked into a pattern which is difficult to change. It is not clear who should take the lead to change the pattern when there is great risk that others will not follow.

Systems change requires leadership of a high moral order. A leader in a system is someone who takes the first steps towards what they deeply care about and in ways that others will wish to follow. A leader creates a path out of the inertia of the system; leaders do not wait for others to initiate the change.

WHEN WILL YOUR
LIFE'S WORK BE DONE

Let your internal vision guide you through life, not the goals set for you by others.

I stopped at a bend in the road. It was early morning. The sun was shining in the Mashobra valley below. I had been walking through the mountain forest for about an hour. I could see the next bend in the road only a few minutes away where there was a small tea shop, a marker by the road to which I had walked yesterday, and the day before. 'If I turn back now I will not have completed my walk,' my mind said.

I sensed the thought of failure forming in my mind, and I wondered, 'How did I choose the tea shop as the marker for completion of my walk?' Perhaps, it was just an arbitrary end point for my walk as the place afforded a pleasant lookout into the valley. Then a deeper question came to my mind. 'What was "it" that I had set out to do when I took off for my walk? Was it the reaching of some milestone? Some amount of exercise? Or was it simply for peace of mind?'

I meet many young people nowadays in their thirties and early forties who have achieved a lot and want to do something different. They have set up successful enterprises and made a fair amount of money already. There are older people too, who have retired after successful, well-paying careers. They tell me they are now looking to 'give back' to society, and to do something more 'meaningful'. They mention the many markers of their achievements yet they feel their life's journey is not done. They want to change course, to take another road, one less taken.

I leaned on my walking stick. The peace in the forest and the mountains induced in me an even deeper reflection. How do we know the 'it'? How do we know when our life's work is really done? Do we consciously and deliberately choose the goals we want to achieve in our lives? Or, do they mostly slip into our minds unconsciously to become markers against which we then measure the satisfactions and dissatisfactions of our lives?

On walking back home, I wondered what purpose an individual human life can fulfil in the grand scheme of things. I happened to be reading a book on Mahatma Gandhi's work and I wondered whether he would have thought his life's work was done when he was assassinated. He had devoted his life to combat injustice and poverty, yet they still persist. So, one may say that Gandhi failed to achieve his goal. On the other hand, most of us would say that Gandhi's work had fulfilled an important purpose in the evolving story of humanity's progress and that his life was a stellar achievement.

Back in my apartment in the mountain village, I pulled up a chair against the window. Looking down into the deep valley with little villages nestled in it, I continued to reflect. I put on a cassette tape of old songs. One was the Ballad of Jimmy Brown—'All the chapel bells were ringing, in the little valley town. And the song that they were singing, was for baby Jimmy Brown.' In the next verse, the chapel bells sing again to celebrate Jimmy Brown's marriage. And then, at last, a lonely chapel bell peals to mark his death. What was the purpose of Jimmy Brown's life? I wondered.

I thought of the local people in my village. The young carpenter and his old father—their family had lived here for a few generations. The village grocer and his family too. In the mountains they were born and in the mountains they have passed away. Their children listen to music on their smartphones: they don't recognize a cassette tape. Though technologies have changed over the centuries, the rhythms of their lives have not. What goals do these people set out to achieve, and what purposes do their lives fulfil? What is 'it' they accomplish, and by what signs do they know 'it' is done?

Doing good work

Looking across the vast valley to the mountains beyond, I wrote some words in my notebook:

I meditate to discover my role in the World's Game
I realize the Eternal is playing its game through me.

Our lives perform certain roles in the functioning of society and our deaths play a role in the sustainability of nature. Each of our lives is a small means for a much larger system to achieve its ends. We have vocations, either chosen by us or assigned to us. When we perform our vocations to the best of our abilities, perhaps we help to make the world a better place for everyone.

Our vocations must transcend into our avocations, the poet Robert Frost urges in his poem *Two Tramps in Mud Time* (which I have quoted from in my story 'What Consultants Really Do'). It is not enough to do one's work faithfully. We should not be like the musician who is satisfied by producing music that only sounds good to others. Rather we should become like a musician who is not satisfied until the music he produces meets the high standards he sets for himself. His vocation must not only be a means of putting money in his bank but also it must satisfy his soul.

Achievement

In Frost's transcendental world, only I may know when I have reached my goal. The world may never know it. This modest view will not satisfy most of us. I want the world to know that I have climbed higher than anyone has so far, that I have run faster than anyone else has, that I am better than others at what I do and, I am the best. We want the world to recognize our achievements. We want to be celebrated all the time. We need the world to felicitate us when we have achieved something worthwhile.

What if someone beats my record while I am still alive? Would that make my life a less successful one?

In this world view my life is successful if I create a world record. But what if someone beats my record while I am still alive (and perhaps many may do), would that make my life a less successful one? Should I then attempt to break the record again before I die to make my life a success again? When, in such a competitive world, will my life's work be done?

Sadly, satisfaction that comes from public adulation is transient. If public recognition is the only way to know when I have 'arrived', I will feel like a failure when the public announces another winner over me and I am demoted from the top spot. The many stories of celebrities who become depressive and even suicidal when they are no longer attractive to the public should be a warning about the dangers in measuring one's success solely through the eyes of others.

I began to read the Bhagavad Gita when I was a teenager, over sixty years ago. I became fixated since then on the lines in the second chapter to which I return again and again. 'You only have a right to the work, and not to the fruits thereof.' The Gita preaches detachment from the fruits of labour. What are the fruits? The obvious interpretation is the benefit one derives for oneself from the work done. What about the achievement of the goal? Is it not a fruit of the work as well? Should one not seek the goal but only strive to do good work and do it well? Is this the meaning of 'right to the work', which is all that one must aim for?

A story from Chris Bonington's compilation of stories of great adventurers and sportsmen that I had read forty years ago, when I was struggling with the lines from the second chapter of the Gita (which I still am), continues to haunt me. It is an account of a round-the-world solo yacht race.

The winner, way ahead of the others, had rounded the tip of South America from the Pacific to the Atlantic Ocean. As he was sailing up towards London, towards the finish line, he heard on his radio of the preparations for his reception. The Queen would come, and the media of course would be there in droves. He thought about it. Was this why he was racing— to reap the fruits of success? Or was it for the love of sailing at its best? He turned his boat around, sailed down the Atlantic and round the Cape of Good Hope into the Indian Ocean to complete another solo circumnavigation of the Earth!

Making the world better

I write a few more lines in my notebook:

> Endless forever the vast water,
> On its surface surges a wave.
> Many have passed and many shall come
> But this is the wave of our times
> And I a ripple on its back.
> As I crest I touch
> The sky of ethereal notions
> And my head encloses
> A little bubble of that infinity too
> Claiming it for my own.

Locked within an infinite universe, which is a vast and very complex system, and being only a very small part of it, we cannot know what the purpose of the whole system is, and what, as it evolves, it is choosing to evolve to. However, we have desires to fulfil, and goals we set out to achieve—whether we consciously chose them or not.

What is the nature of these goals? They can be goals of achievements that society recognizes and rewards—goals that one adopts, which are not intrinsic to ourselves. Or, they can be goals of self-perfection (as Frost implies). They could also be goals of self-realization (which many spiritual and meditative traditions recommend).

However, there is another type of journey that some leaders undertake to achieve another type of goal. It is the journey Mahatma Gandhi set out on. He wanted to make the world a haven for people who had been poor and suppressed for generations. He was not competing for honours. Nor was he satisfied with meditations and self-purification, though he pursued these goals too. He wanted to bring about a change in the world, not just in himself. Leaders like Gandhi are conscious that they are part of a much larger ocean with large waves that sweep through it. However, they are not megalomaniacs, like King Canute, to command the tide to turn. They strive to understand the nature of the ocean and the sources of its power. They strive also to improve their own abilities to change the pattern of the tides. Most of all, they engage in action. Their lives are a combination of reflection, insight and action. No wonder Gandhi called his autobiography, *The Story of My Experiments with Truth*.

Leaders who want to transform society, with its complexities, and go against the momentum of its history to make the world a sanctuary for everyone, cannot accomplish their goals in their lifetimes. Yet some devote their lives to this mission, and even surrender their lives to it, as did Jesus, who gave his life on the cross to redeem mankind. Although Jesus's sacrifice did not complete the mission in his lifetime, it did give his mission an enormous thrust. The message of his life continues to reverberate around the world.

Gandhi was inspired by the story of Jesus. He referred to the Bible and to the Bhagavad Gita throughout his life. Inspired by Gandhi, I too read the Gita. The lines in the second chapter, which I have mentioned earlier, continue to haunt me—'You only have a right to the work, and not to the fruits thereof.' Great leaders, even those as great as Gandhi and Jesus, cannot create the change they aspire for in their own lifetimes because the world is complex and many forces must interact to change the world. If the only reason to perform a task was to enjoy its fruits, there would have been no motivation for these great men to undertake missions that could not be completed in their own lifetimes. Yet they persisted.

Because complex changes are produced by many forces coming together, no single action or person can claim credit for it

There is further wisdom in those words in the Gita. Because complex changes and their fruits are produced by many forces coming together, no single action nor any one person can claim to be the sole producer of the fruit. Even Mahatma Gandhi and Jesus Christ are only a part of a larger process. There was history before them; and there is history after them too.

I write another thought in my notebook:

When I sit by the water
The waves pass unremembered,
The ripples unnoticed
Like my momentary existence.

We must be humble suggests the Gita. If we are fortunate to be at the helm of affairs—be on the choicest branch of the tree as it were—when the fruit ripens, we must not claim all of it. We must be humble, because the fruit was produced by the efforts of many. The Gita's lesson of the 'right to the work and not its fruits', and of the humility that must come with it, has been lost in the present mad increases in CEO compensation. Nowadays, CEOs earn many hundreds of times more than the average salaries of people in their own organizations, whereas, thirty years ago, CEOs used to earn only dozens of times more. The justification given by CEOs (and executive search firms—who too are beneficiaries when levels of executive compensation rise) is that those who produce the results must be given a 'fair' share of the same so that they are motivated to do their best. However, 'fairness' cannot justify paying CEOs so much more than they were being paid before. They were certainly not a deprived lot earlier, when too they had much more than others to satisfy their needs.

If 'fairness' cannot provide a moral justification for the sharp increase in the proportion of fruit claimed by those at the top of the tree, 'adequacy' of compensation is an even weaker justification. For those who earn 10 crores of rupees a year, to even suggest that they 'need' another few crores seems obscene. It is also insulting to those who live quite happily on a few lakhs a year.

Choosing the game we want to play

Great leaders choose to focus on the purpose of the enterprise more than the profit it makes. Their goal in life is not to make more wealth and fame for themselves but to increase the well-being of society.

On the portals of the Military Academy in Dehradun, from which Indian Army officers, who lead men even to give up their own lives in service of their country, pass out, is a sign that says, 'For when the One Great Scorer comes to write against your name, He writes—not that you won or lost—but how you played the game.'

We can choose the kind of game we want to play with our lives and the types of rewards we desire. The rule book of life is unlike long-distance running and the World Wrestling Federation's contests which are different types of games—with different goals, different rules and different ways of keeping score.

Many successful people I meet say that they want to improve their work–life balance. I often think there is an imbalance in their means–ends equation. They focus on achievement of ends (wealth, size of their organization, fame) that society measures and applauds, and devote too little attention to the means. Companies burn up the environment to create more profits and shareholder value, and people burn out to stay ahead of others in the rat race.

Wealth and popularity are visible markers of success in the game of life, but if these become overriding measures of the worthiness of a person's life, then they demand more of it than others to be successful, no matter how well they live their life. With such markers, it is the quantity of one's *having* rather than the quality of one's *being* that determine the games one will play with one's life.

Who we choose as our role models shape what we want to be and how we want to live our lives. Are they people who have achieved a lot of wealth and popularity? Or, are they those who strive on, with evidently no personal gain, towards self-prescribed goals and progress towards an end that cannot be mechanically measured by society's conventional scorecards?

The young, high achievers, by conventional standards, who tell me they are missing 'something' in their lives are searching for another type of game to play, which has different goals. They must drop out of the mass race (the rat race?) with its public drumbeats egging on the competition. They must march to a different drum, the beats of which only they may hear. The markers of progress to their goals will not be visible to those who do not know the goals of the journey they are on. Only they will know when they have attained the standards they have set for themselves. Such journeys can be lonely; but they are worthwhile. They can be deeply satisfying for the traveller. And they can help to make the world better for everyone.

(P.S. After writing down these reflections, I went out for another walk. This time I walked up to the tea stall, and beyond it—just for the heck of it!)

LEARNING, LISTENING,
SYSTEMS THINKING

AN ODD CONSULTANT

Consultants can help their clients better by listening to real people, in real places, than by analysing spreadsheets of numbers.

The managing directors (MDs) at ADL Inc., the consulting company in the US that had hired me in 1989, believed I had the potential to be a good management consultant. However, they had a problem convincing their clients. I was forty-five years old and had worked all my life with Indian manufacturing companies, viz. Tata Steel and Tata Engineering and Locomotive Company. Moreover, I did not even have a management degree. What value would any US company, even one in the manufacturing sector, expect to get from the advice of a senior Indian manager, even if he had been successful in India?

When I arrived in the USA in 1989, US manufacturing companies were churning as Japanese manufacturers were providing US customers with far better and less expensive products in industries like automobiles, consumer electronics, household appliances, chemical products, etc. Many US companies, unable to compete with the Japanese, were downsizing and closing their factories. When companies are in trouble, they hire consultants to either help them reduce their costs or to turn them around. This created an opportunity for ADL to sell its services.

Japanese industries had recovered remarkably after their devastation in the Second World War. The 'secret ingredient' that all Japanese companies used, whatever their product or technology, was called Total Quality Management (TQM). I had learnt the whole recipe from Japanese companies.

TQM was an overall philosophy of continuous improvement. Toyota had adopted it (called it the Toyota Production System) and so did other companies. TQM is a set of principles for systems improvement introduced by Prof. William Edwards Deming. It is also a set of simple tools for problem-solving developed by Prof. Kaoru Ishikawa that workers can use to improve work processes and reduce wastage of time, materials and energy. Indeed, this new Japanese approach to management, with which Japan Inc. was beating US Inc., was so profound and yet so simple that when US company executives went to study the secret of Japan's success, and were told what the secret was, they complained the Japanese were hiding something!

TQM eliminated the need for expensive quality inspections and also the need for buffer stocks because workers were motivated to make improvements, and they were equipped to do this with the tools of TQM. Production processes became so reliable that the outcome required would always come out error-free and on time: there was no need to inspect or rework.

In western industrial countries, there was a belief that workers cannot be relied upon to do things correctly, therefore experts in industrial engineering are required to lay down rules; a hierarchy of supervisors is necessary to make them work; inspectors are essential to check for quality of products; and buffers are essential to maintain continuity of production because there would be many failures regardless of the controls. The difference between the western and the Japanese approaches to management was that, in the West, workers were assumed to be inherently lazy, generally untrustworthy, perhaps even unintelligent, whereas, in the Japanese approach, engaging the workers was the management's secret ingredient for improving quality and reducing costs.

Books on TQM began to appear in the West in the 1980s. Many were written by Japanese consultants. Japanese industry also began to open up to foreigners, inviting them to learn how Japanese companies worked. Prof. Masaaki Imai was a well-known Japanese consultant, famous for his work on 'kaizen'—a Japanese term meaning 'change for the better'. Kaizen, following the TQM philosophy, involves all employees in a process of continuous improvement. Prof. Imai invited thirty senior executives from international companies to Japan in 1981, (for a hefty fee, though!) for a two-week study tour. Mr Sumant Moolgaokar, the chairman of TELCO, where I was employed at the time, was invited too. However, he felt he was too old to travel and deputed me to go instead, on the condition that I would take extensive notes and circulate a detailed report to all senior officers of TELCO when I returned.

My visit to Japan turned around my ideas of good business management. The thirty exclusive invitees were from many countries, mostly from the USA and from Europe. There was only one other person from India, a CEO from a large industrial group. Prof. Imai, our host and a respected consultant in Japan, arranged for us to meet Prof. Ishikawa, who was already becoming a living legend in Japan. We were also invited to inspect the factories of Toyota, Hitachi, Mitsubishi and other renowned Japanese companies, and to meet with their engineers and senior managers too. In our hunt for the 'TQM secrets', we could ask them for clues.

Seeds of TQM began to spread in India around that time, especially in the auto and auto parts industries. On returning from Japan, I submitted my report to Moolgaokar and he circulated it among senior executives in the company. More pertinently, he asked me how I intended to apply what I had learnt to improve our operations.

Immediately, a drive to introduce the methods of TQM began in TELCO Pune. Selected engineers were trained to be facilitators. Dozens of 'quality circles', in which workers met every week to plan improvements in their departments, sprouted around the factory. Periodically the best quality circles were invited to share their work with others. Thus, TELCO's factories in Pune became infected with TQM enthusiasm. Other companies around Pune followed suit.

TQM became contagious. I was elected by the local industries as the first president of the Quality Circle movement in Pune.

The movement caught on in other parts of the country, especially in Chennai and Bangalore where there were a large number of auto parts producers and suppliers to TELCO. The Maruti car company near Delhi that had begun operations in collaboration with Suzuki Japan introduced TQM methods to Maruti and its suppliers. Soon there were national competitions amongst quality circles from different parts of the country.

Auto parts producers in India took up TQM most vigorously. They were always under pressure from the original equipment manufacturers (OEMs), like TELCO and Maruti, to improve the quality and reliability of their supplies and to reduce costs at the same time. TQM gave them the tools to do it. Many Indian auto parts producers improved so much that they began to successfully export to the USA.

ADL had set up a TQM consulting practice to serve the US companies that were beginning to realize that they had to apply Japanese methods to compete with the Japanese companies that had begun to swarm into the USA. ADL presented me to its potential clients as a leader of its practice with hands-on experience of introducing TQM into manufacturing companies, albeit far away in India.

Soon after I had settled down in the USA, I went with an ADL team to make a pitch to a US auto parts producer that was a principal supplier to the Big Three in the US—GM, Ford Motor Company and Chrysler. The company was in big trouble. The OEMs were under pressure to improve their quality of manufacturing at reduced costs to compete with Toyota, Nissan and Honda that claimed large shares of the US market with their high-quality, low-price cars. The US OEMs wanted better performance and lower costs of parts from their own suppliers, many of which were unable to withstand the pressure and were forced to close down or sell out.

A German engineering conglomerate was considering the purchase of the US parts producer where ADL went to make a pitch. The German company had been warned that old plants in the US could have large liabilities under US laws which could be a big burden for new owners. There were environmental 'clean up' costs to clear out toxins from the land and water around old factories which may have operated for many years with old equipment before new stringent environmental regulations came into force. Also, there were costs for 'downsizing' the workforce—compensation to be paid to workers and pensions too. ADL was asked by the German buyer to make an assessment of these costs before it finalized the purchase.

The German company was prepared to bear the environmental costs, if they were not unreasonable, but it was concerned about the political backlash in America against a foreign company buying a US company and then firing a large number of its employees. Loss of jobs due to global competition was already becoming a political issue. The Germans wanted ADL to evaluate whether, and also how, the company could be run profitably with a minimum number of job losses. That is where my expertise would be valuable,

ADL proposed, with my knowledge of the TQM approach in which workers were not costs but sources of improvement.

The US company had three plants. The ones in Philadelphia and Detroit were very old and were the sources of concern. I had to evaluate the plants' costs as well as the potential in their workforces. Two young consultants, with degrees in engineering from MIT (perhaps the world's best engineering school), who also had degrees from US business schools, were assigned to work with me. They were razor-sharp with their numbers and their assessments of the state of technology in the plants. However, their tools of management and engineering were not designed for making an assessment of the human potential in the plants.

The time assigned in the consulting contract for making assessments of the plants was limited. Where was I most likely to find clues about the state of human affairs? I volunteered to come in for the night shift.

The plant manager in Philadelphia, the first plant I undertook to assess, was alarmed. The plant was in a run-down part of Philadelphia, where poor, and mostly black people lived. The managers of the plant lived in the suburbs of Philadelphia and drove in and out during daytime. Workers on the night shift mostly lived in the neighbourhood. The area around the plant was a dangerous one, the manager warned me. Shootings and muggings were common. If I would like to observe the night shift, as I insisted, the manager recommended that I come in with the earlier shift at daylight, stay through the night, and return to my hotel only in the morning. I could have dinner in the workers' cafeteria, though he apologized for the quality of the food. Alternatively, I could bring my own sandwich if I liked to. I decided to take my chances with the workers.

Actually, very few workers ate in the small, dingy cafeteria. The workers on the earlier shift went home to eat and those on the night shift had already eaten at home before coming in. When I went into the cafe, the large black woman behind the tiny counter was surprised to see a strange man— not black, and not quite white either. I saw apprehension in her eyes. Fortunately for her, there was a large black man seated at one table in the cafe. He had a soda can in his hand. He looked at me and greeted me. 'Say, are you the consultant they said was coming around to see if we folks are good enough?'

I sensed some animosity in his eyes as well as in his tone. But there was a hint of curiosity too because I didn't match his image of a consultant.

I admitted I was the consultant. 'Geez, where you from?' the woman asked. 'From India,' I replied. 'India!' both exclaimed together. That broke the ice. The man was on the night shift and he recommended what I might eat from the very limited stuff in the cafe. I joined him at the table and told him and the lady how I had come all the way from India to Philadelphia.

He escorted me to the factory where I was given a chair to sit on in the supervisor's cubicle next to the production line. The supervisor walked me through the line and explained the production process. He told the workers that I was the consultant their union had warned them would come snooping around. I sensed the same combination of animosity and curiosity that had lit up my companion in the cafe.

During the long night hours, with machines clanging outside, several workers came into the supervisor's cubicle to talk to me. Sometimes the supervisor was present, sometimes he was not. The workers asked about me, and I had questions for them. They told me that their managers seemed barely interested in them; they lived in another world altogether.

Many workers had been with the plant for decades—from the company's good days into its bad times in the last few years. They had seen managers come and go while they had stayed on. When they realized that I understood their production technology—in fact the equipment in the TELCO factories was more advanced—they began to explain to me what the bottlenecks were. The supervisor joined in and told me that he had pleaded with the management for small investments with which production could be increased and wastage of material and energy reduced as well. But the requests were turned down. His managers said he was making excuses for not being able to get his workers to work harder. The suggestions of workers for small changes were dismissed too by the college-educated engineers who came to evaluate the production line. They had concluded that the technology was too old to salvage. And the finance department said there was no money to make the large investments the engineers envisaged. So, the company was up for sale.

The company's workers were members of a labour union, the United Auto Workers (UAW). The sale of the company, as well as the downsizing of its factories, would require the support of the union. Whereas relations between employers and unions in the US were generally adversarial, German industries had a more cooperative culture. The union in Philadelphia asked the prospective German buyer for a meeting to present its plan for saving the plant by improving productivity and quality with many suggestions that had come from the workers. The plan would require cooperation from management with investments recommended by the union. The German company agreed to hear the union's alternative plan.

The union had begun to have trust in ADL after my night visits and conversations with workers in the old plants in Philadelphia and Detroit. The union asked ADL for help to improve its plan and validate the financial numbers. The two young ADL consultants from MIT assisted the union.

In the meeting with the management, the industrial engineering experts from the headquarters tried to find loopholes in the union's plan. However, the ADL consultants assisting the union understood technology and the math of finance as well as the staff engineers did. Finally, a deal between the union and the engineers was struck—fewer jobs would be cut and investments would be made. The plan's progress would be reviewed by the management and the union together to ensure that both sides were keeping to their commitments and that the outcomes expected were being achieved. Thus, the plant was kept open for many more years, and some of the workers on the night shift, who would have lost their jobs with the plan the management had proposed earlier, could continue to come to work and earn, as well as see their ideas being implemented.

The success of ADL's intervention with the auto parts supplier to the OEMs attracted the attention of managers in the automobile OEMs. Ford invited ADL to apply the TQM approach in one of its own plants.

The Ford Motor Company, and its legendary founder, Henry Ford I, was the pioneer of many ideas in industrial management. These included the assembly line in auto production, time-motion-based industrial engineering and mass production of complex products like automobiles. The Ford Model T put middle-class America on wheels. It was far less expensive than its competitor's cars because it was a mass-produced, standardized car. 'Any customer can have a car painted any colour that he wants so long as it is black,' Henry Ford had quipped.

Henry Ford was a generous paymaster. He unilaterally doubled the wages of the workers in his plants and upset the salary structure of the automobile industry. He defended his action saying he wanted his workers to be able to buy his cars and thus to expand the market for cars. He was able to reduce overall costs by standardizing the parts of the car and systematizing the production line.

The Ford factory in Dearborn was the 'machine that changed the world' in the early part of the twentieth century. It was a completely integrated plant. The iron ore came off barges on Lake Michigan directly into the blast furnaces— the plant even made its own steel! —the steel was machined into parts, and the parts were assembled by workers at long assembly lines, and out came a Ford Model T at the other end of the line.

Henry Ford complained that when he wanted only a pair of hands in the factory, he would get a whole human being with emotions and feelings. Industrial engineers could programme the motions of hands, to save time and cost in production, but they could not control the feelings of the workers, who resented being treated like robots. Violent fights erupted between unionized workers and management's security teams in the Ford factory, resulting in many deaths.

In 1991, Prof. James P. Womack of MIT wrote a book *The Machine that Changed the World.* The subtitle was, *The Story of Lean Production—Toyota's Secret Weapon in the Global Car Wars that Is Now Revolutionizing World Industry.* His book told the story of how small-scale Japanese automobile producers were outsmarting the big US competitors. Womack consulted with ADL (which had emerged from MIT in the late nineteenth century and there were close associations between the two institutions) when he was completing his book. I got to know him quite well then.

The Ford Motor Company was determined to decode the secret of the Japanese companies and catch up with them. It engaged Prof. Joseph M. Juran, the American engineer and management consultant who had become the evangelist for quality management in the US in the early 1990s, to advise Ford on a company-wide programme of quality improvement. Juran's approach to quality was the same as the Japanese approach to TQM: Everyone must be involved in improving quality—from the top management to workers, not just the industrial engineers and quality inspectors. (Ford had also hired ADL to apply TQM in one of its plants, as I have mentioned earlier.)

One day, while I was working in the Ford plant, Public Broadcasting Service (PBS), the national public television channel, announced it was interviewing Prof. Juran about whether US industry was learning fast enough to catch up with its Japanese competitors who were not standing still but continuously improving. The managers in the plant assembled in the conference room where I joined them to hear Prof. Juran speak.

There is a widespread belief that consultants must be proficient with numbers and spreadsheets and that they must be brutally 'objective' and stick to the facts. In fact, data analytics is becoming one of the fastest-growing disciplines in management consulting. But Prof. Juran painted another picture.

The interviewer asked Juran, who was in his nineties then, whether Americans would catch up with the Japanese. Juran seemed overwhelmed with emotions when he replied, 'They don't get it. Quality is not in the numbers. It is in the people.'

SPEAKING THE SAME LANGUAGE

Even young consultants can learn to be great coaches to clients.

Two ADL consultants and I were waiting in a minibus at the Guadalajara International Airport in Mexico for three other consultants to join us. We all worked in the same international management consulting company, ADL Inc., but the three of us on the bus had never met the three we were waiting for. They were flying in from Spain; I had flown in from the USA the evening before. At dinner, I had met the two consultants from ADL's offices in Mexico City and Monterrey, one of whom, Carlos, was the designated project leader. He was the only one of the five ADL consultants with whom I had worked before. The six of us would travel to the hills where Cemex, the giant Mexican cement company, had one of its fourteen plants. The other plants were spread around the country, most of them in remote locations close to deposits of limestone to feed their cement-manufacturing kilns.

I was the only one who did not speak Spanish. On the bus, Carlos and the others opened their computers. He ran them through some slides that he had mailed them before they took off from Madrid. The slides were in Spanish. We were told that only one person spoke English in the plant we were travelling to. Therefore, business would be conducted entirely in Spanish.

A few months before, I had waited for several hours in the office of the CEO of Cemex, along with four colleagues from ADL: the CEO of ADL, the MD of ADL's Mexico operations, and two colleagues from my consulting team in the US. We had come to make our pitch to Cemex's CEO, Lorenzo Zambrano, on whose instructions Cemex had put out a global RFP (request for proposals) to consulting companies who could help Cemex fulfil Zambrano's ambition to make Cemex 'the Toyota of the cement industry'.

Zambrano's family were the principal shareholders of Cemex. He was a 'cement man'. He had worked in the cement plants and 'had the grey stuff in his blood', as he confidently told us when we met. Cemex was a powerhouse in Mexico. It dominated the domestic cement industry. However, since Mexico had recently signed the NAFTA pact (the North American Free Trade Agreement) with the USA and Canada, Mexican companies would have to face tough competition from much larger US companies from across the border. The only way to survive, Zambrano declared, was to become the most efficient producer of cement in the world, just as Toyota, having become the most efficient automobile producer in the world, was now venturing successfully into the US market beating larger US companies on their home turf.

Zambrano wanted Cemex to become a 'faster learning organization', so that it could catch up with the best in the world and stay ahead of them, because they too would be continuously improving. Cemex itself had been upgrading year on year. Now it would have to accelerate the speed of its learning. The evidence of faster learning would be the rate at which Cemex plants improved their hard performance parameters: their cost of production, the uptime of their equipment, and the reliability of their deliveries—the stuff of good manufacturing management.

A team of Cemex executives had already examined the proposals received from the many consulting companies that were enticed by the mouth-watering prospect of a huge multi-year contract. They had interviewed half a dozen consulting companies in Houston and had shortlisted three of them. Team ADL sent to Houston to make the pitch in the preliminaries was led by ADL's most successful consultant in manufacturing process improvement. He made an extremely convincing case about ADL's ability to improve plant performance parameters. The Cemex executives were impressed, hence we were shortlisted for the final interview with Zambrano.

Zambrano was known to be a tough CEO who expected high performance from his plant managers. He wanted to meet the three finalists and approve the winner. ADL was one them, so we were anxiously waiting for our interview with Zambrano.

During the meetings in Houston, it became evident to all the consultants who were interviewed that Zambrano was personally very serious about 'learning management', not just manufacturing management. Therefore, ADL's manufacturing expert felt it would be prudent to bring along other consultants for the finals with Zambrano. One of them was Dr Jayakumar, a consultant in organization behaviour, who was a senior-level lateral hire into ADL, like I was, and also a member of ADL's organizational consulting practice.

I was there at the meeting too. I had recently moved from ADL's organization practice to lead ADL's manufacturing management practice to bring the 'people' side into manufacturing management, the benefits of which I had demonstrated in ADL's work with US auto companies that were rapidly learning TQM to try to catch up with the likes of Toyota Japan. The MD of our Mexico operations, who was very keen to win the contract, insisted I come. He also persuaded the CEO of ADL, Dr Charles LaMantia, to come down to assure Zambrano that ADL would pull out all stops and deploy its best resources in the world to serve Cemex if we won the contract. (Which he had to do when we won the contract. Hence the best young consultants from Spain were on the flight from Madrid to Guadalajara that morning.)

Zambrano made us wait for over two hours. When he came into the room, he was clearly impatient. Our manufacturing expert began his presentation. He started to list all the improvements that could be made in the two Cemex plants he had visited earlier to carry out a diagnostic while preparing for the meeting with Zambrano. Zambrano stopped him abruptly. 'I already know all that; don't bore me,' he said. 'I want to know what is going on in the workers' minds. Don't talk to me about the grey powder that flows through the cement plant. I want to know about the grey matter inside the workers' minds. Do they know these are improvements that could be made? Do they care?'

When our manufacturing expert responded that the workers and managers in the plant evidently did not know or care enough and hence these improvements had not been made so far—he thought he was justifying Cemex's need for experts like him—Zambrano suddenly got up to leave! Our Mexican MD pleaded with Zambrano to give us a few more minutes since our CEO had flown in specially to meet him. Zambrano sat down again and said he would give us only a few minutes.

Dr Jayakumar, who was a very short man, about 5 feet 3 inches tall, dark-brown complexioned, with a straggly black beard, and who looked like an Indian yogi in an ill-fitting blue suit, walked right up to Zambrano and looked him in his eyes. 'Changing the culture of an organization is like turning around an elephant,' he said. 'I know because I have learnt to turn around real elephants in the state of Mysore from where I come. Until elephants want to turn, they will continue to resist your prodding.'

He had clearly hooked Zambrano who was eager to hear more. Dr Jayakumar and I then laid out the strategy for Cemex that he and I had devised when we had learnt about the type of consulting Zambrano was looking for. We told him that we would begin work on the 'human side' of the enterprise, which would eventually take charge of the 'technical side' of the enterprise—people first; technological improvements would follow. We explained our principles of work and cited examples of how and where we had applied them.

Zambrano was impressed with ADL. He had already approved one other consulting company for the job. Since the task to be accomplished in Cemex was huge—fourteen plants in remote locations to be engaged and improved quickly—Cemex's executives advised him that it would be best to not put all their eggs in one basket. He agreed. ADL was assigned all the plants in one of the three regions that the fourteen plants were categorized into; the other consulting company was assigned all the plants in another region; while the third region, that was not convinced that any of the consulting companies knew as yet how to apply esoteric concepts like 'organization learning' to the nitty-gritty of cement plants, said they would wait it out to see how the other regions progressed with their consultants.

The contract was that in three months' time Zambrano and the heads of all three divisions would assess the progress made by the two consulting companies and decide what the further course of action would be. It could even be to terminate the consulting engagements altogether if they were not found satisfactory.

ADL came out ahead. The region that had initially chosen to work with the other consultant said it wanted to switch to ADL. And the third region, which had been observing from the side, also asked ADL for help. This spurred a sudden need to enlarge the ADL team considerably and to find Spanish-speaking consultants from around the world to supplement the resources within ADL in Mexico.

Carlos had distilled, simply and elegantly, the principles of engagement that had worked well so far. He described the steps to be taken, day-wise, in the first week. On the last day of the week, all managers and representatives of workers would gather together with the consultants to collectively review the possibilities for the plant. In this meeting, they would outline their aspirations for change. The managers would report their honest assessment of the current reality and its distance from their aspiration. Following which the ADL team would describe the participative process whereby ADL consultants could help the Cemex team to achieve its own aspirations.

After the conclusion of the meeting, the consultants would leave, and the plant manager would ask his team whether they would like to work with ADL. He would then convey his plant's decision to the regional manager, and ADL would return to the plant only if they were invited again.

Before we reached the plant, Carlos confirmed that all the consultants were on the same page about the steps to be taken that week and everyone was equally enthusiastic.

The same process of participative assessment was applied in all plants. There were fourteen plants to overhaul now, whereas there were only three just a few months ago. The number of Spanish-speaking consultants required to staff the Cemex project had increased greatly. ADL's Mexico offices went into a crash recruitment drive. Freshers, mostly MBAs, who were new to consulting joined the ADL team.

Dr Jayakumar organized training programmes to induct them into the people-centred approach to performance improvement that ADL was deploying. The consultants working in the various plants would meet together periodically to compare notes and improve their own consulting methods and capabilities. Since all the consultants spoke English as well as Spanish, Dr Jayakumar and I could facilitate these learning meetings.

The first step of engagement in every plant was to ask all stakeholders what benefits they expected if the plant were to be transformed. A worker in the plant near Guadalajara had said he hoped the plant would become so clean that his wife would not have to work so hard to wash the grey dust off his work clothes. 'She has to work hard cooking and caring for the children,' he said, 'it breaks my heart to see her scrubbing my filthy clothes every night.'

Making the plant clean required better maintenance of the machinery and advanced pollution control equipment too. This would prevent both wastage of materials and health hazards of workers. Low cost and low pollution, the metrics of 'world-class' plant performance, were aligned with the life needs of workers. They could clearly see the benefits of Zambrano's mission of making Cemex a global benchmark.

When Dr Jayakumar had confronted Zambrano in the first momentous meeting in his office, he had asked Zambrano, looking him in the eye, why he wanted to embark on such a large and risky transformation programme. In addition to the necessity of the survival of the company, Zambrano said he wanted Mexico to be respected.

With the rapid improvements in the performance of Cemex's cement plants, Zambrano realized his vision. Starting from its home base in Mexico, where Cemex had felt vulnerable to international competition with the signing of the NAFTA trade agreement, it rapidly grew to become one of the three largest cement companies in the world with operations in many countries. Zambrano's picture appeared on the covers of international news magazines with the story of how Cemex, a Mexican cement company, had become one of the most admired cement companies in the world.

Zambrano's ambition for rapid transformation could not have been achieved if his ambition for the company was not aligned with the aspirations of the workers for the improvements they wanted in their working conditions. He had known this well when he told the ADL team that he was not concerned about the grey stuff that flowed through the cement process. He wanted to know what was going on in the 'grey matter' inside workers' minds.

The insights into practical methods for engaging all stakeholders that the consultants learnt during the Cemex transformation, as well as insights from several other consulting engagements in many industries, were compiled into a book. At the urging of our colleagues in ADL, Dr Peter Scott-Morgan and I wrote *The Accelerating Organization: Embracing the Human Face of Change,* which was published by McGraw Hill in 1996.

This was my first book. My second book, *Shaping the Future: Aspirational Leadership in India and Beyond,* published by John Wiley & Sons in 2002, was prompted by the Boston

Consulting Group that I had joined as the chairman of their India consulting practice on my return to India in 2000. This book was inspired by another consulting engagement—to describe the path to the future of my own country, India. That is another story.

A CONSULTANT IN THE ROOM

Consultants listen carefully to their clients; good consultants enable their clients to listen to others; and the best consultants help their clients to listen to their own hearts.

Tata Tea's acquisition of the Tetley tea company in the UK was the first of the three high-profile acquisitions of British companies by the Tata Group in the first decade of the twenty-first century. The other two were the Jaguar Land Rover car company and the Corus steel company (formerly known as British Steel). The acquisitions were hailed as the reversal of the tide of industrial colonialization of India in the nineteenth century, when Britain took raw materials from India, such as cotton, iron ore and tea, processed them in its factories, and exported the finished products around the world. British workers earned good salaries doing high-skilled 'value-adding' jobs, and British companies made lots of profits. In a turn in history, the Tata Group, which acquired iconic British companies, was hailed as a saviour of British blue-collar jobs.

The Tetley tea company was founded in 1837 by Joseph and Edward Tetley. Its different flavours of tea became well known wherever tea was savoured around the world, especially in the rich European and American countries. By the turn of the millennium, Indian companies had become cash-rich following a decade of heady growth with the opening of the Indian economy after the momentous economic reforms in 1991. On the other hand, British manufacturing companies had been limping along for years as the British economy veered towards the financialization of its economy, making Britain the centre of financial innovation in the world, while neglecting the 'blue-collar' sectors of its economy that had made Britain an industrial powerhouse in the nineteenth century.

Cross-cultural mergers and acquisitions are never easy. In fact, research in business history shows that they often destroy shareholder value. The business synergies that appear attractive on paper—such as the combination of raw material and production assets of one company and wider access to markets and popular brands of the other—do not materialize in practice. This is because the clash of egos and cultures generates a lot of internal heat and wastes a lot of management energy. Such friction arises even when the two companies are from the same country where national histories and national pride do not further complicate a difficult marriage. But when the two companies come from different nations, their amalgamation can be fraught with complications, as the marriage of two persons from different cultures can be—which is the reason why families caution young people to beware when they venture into marriages outside their own cultures.

Great leaders are aware that when the aspirations of the people in the organization cannot be realized, they are unlikely to give their best for attaining the organization's big numerical targets. They will not just do and die; they will question why.

The Tata Group top management, nurtured in its long history of human-centred management, was aware that strategies are not created from spreadsheets. More importantly, the implementation of a strategy, no matter how rationally sound, cannot be achieved by numbers alone. It is the people in the organization who have to implement the strategy. Therefore, the alignment of the strategy with their aspirations is essential so that not only the numerical goals are achieved but it also fulfils people's expectations of what they want to achieve in their lives.

Tata's top management understood that what they were buying with their money were insights into international marketing of tea, skills in buying and blending the best teas from around the world to satisfy customers in western markets, and the relations Tetley had with its distributors. Such 'intangibles' cannot be packaged into tangible pieces of intellectual property that can be traded in a market. Such intangible and tacit knowledge resides within people. Therefore, Tatas retained most of the top managers and employees of Tetley as an intact team to continue to drive the international business supported by Tatas in India.

The purchase of Tetley, a British company, was a source of great national pride to all Indians, and to the employees of

Tata Tea too. Tetley now belonged to Indians; Indians were the bosses. The international significance of the purchase of a proud British company by an Indian company was noted in the British media.

When a team from the finance department in Tata went to the UK to take stock of the numbers there, they were made to wait in the reception of Tetley's headquarters for their appointment with the British managing director. They were impatient. The British receptionist explained that the boss was busy and would see them shortly. One of the Indians remarked loudly to another that 'she does not know who the boss is now'.

The strategy of the acquisition was sound. However, the chemistry between the teams clearly was not.

I received an urgent request one day from the vice chairman of Tata Tea, who was the mastermind of the Tetley acquisition, to meet him in his office in the Taj Mahal Hotel in Mumbai. He was also the vice chairman of the Indian Hotels Company Limited (IHCL) which owned the Taj Mahal Hotel as well as many other hotels in India and abroad. He and I were former colleagues in the Tata Administrative Services (TAS) where I had served for twenty-five years before I became a consultant with ADL in the USA. I had come to India as chairman of the Boston Consulting Group in India and he wanted to consult me about how he could make the Indian and the British sides of the merged enterprise work as one team with common goals. The two groups had been thrashing out their plans together in the Taj Hotel for two days. There was too much friction, he feared.

I suggested to him that the two groups should have a 'heart-to-heart' meeting rather than a 'numbers-to-numbers' meeting, which management meetings are mostly about. Both the groups should release their suppressed feelings, talk about their aspirations, about what the success of the joint enterprise will mean for each of them and for their personal feelings of fulfilment and self-respect, as well as the kind of respect they want from their peers and their community.

My friend seized the moment. The whole team of eight, from India and the UK, was in the hotel. 'Can you facilitate this meeting tomorrow please?' he pressed me. I checked my calendar. I told him that I could free myself the next day and I wanted to help. I insisted the setting of the meeting had to be a relaxed one; not in a conference room with the chairman at the head of the table. It should be in a living room, with everyone sitting in a circle, in comfortable chairs or sofas, preferably in a room with windows and with space for the participants to move around. The setting of the room should be different to the ones in which they have been conducting their business meetings, to get them out of their ruts and into the spirit of an un-businesslike meeting in which they can talk about what really matters to them as human beings. 'You are in the best place in the world for such a meeting, my friend!' I was assured.

It is widely believed that Jamsetji Tata decided to build the Taj Mahal Hotel in 1900 after he was refused entry to Watson's Hotel, one of Mumbai's (or Bombay, as it was known then) grand hotels of the time as it was restricted to 'whites only'. However, this story has been challenged.

Another story is that the Taj was built at the urging of the then editor of the *Times of India* who felt a hotel 'worthy of Bombay' was needed, as Tata's 'gift to the city he loved'. The Taj opened its doors in 1903. It is one of the finest luxury hotels in the world. Pictures of princes, celebrities and heads of state who have stayed in it are displayed in its lobbies.

The manager of the Taj was summoned and we marched up to the presidential suite. 'Will this do?' the manager asked. The suite was huge with more than one room where we could have our meeting. He urged me to pick the largest and the most plushly furnished one. All participants would be able to sit on comfortable sofas he pointed out. I accepted his suggestion.

'What other arrangements do you want, sir?' the manager asked. 'Tea, coffee, snacks, lunch? There will be a butler in the suite at your service. Anything else?'

I looked around. It was a great setting for the type of meeting I intended. 'I would like an easel with flip charts, and some marker pens,' I said. The manager looked a bit confused. That was an unusual item for meetings of dignitaries in such a grand room. My friend, the manager's boss, had instructed him to make sure I was provided whatever I wanted, and with that we left.

The next morning I came to the hotel half an hour before the meeting to check the arrangements. I was escorted into the room by an assistant manager of the hotel who had been assigned to ensure that everything was in order. When we entered, I was horrified to see that the sofas had been rearranged to make space for a huge screen on one side with a projector on a beautiful coffee table in the middle. The big screen completely dwarfed the small easel with charts, which was the only item I had wanted!

I was dismayed at this overnight conversion. The lovely setting for a heart-to-heart meeting was transformed into a makeshift arrangement for a conventional business meeting. 'Why the screen and the projector?' I asked.

'Because I was told a consultant was conducting the meeting!' he explained. I understood his reasoning. However, I requested him to quickly restore the room to its original configuration and to leave just the low-tech, humble flip chart for me. Out went the screen and the projector.

I find a flip chart a good tool to facilitate dialogues. When there are many participants in a conversation, they often worry that others may not have listened to them properly. Or that, even if they have heard, they will forget as the conversation moves on. So, the speakers often repeat what they had said, anxious that their point is not lost. They may even stop listening to what others are saying, to look for openings to repeat themselves.

I like to note the important points that people make on the flip chart. There, they are visible to all and on record. Moreover, if I do not record a point correctly, the speaker can correct me. Thus, by dwelling on important points, the group is able to absorb them too. In an hour or two of discussion, everyone feels they have been heard. Then I make the group pause, and run through the notes on the flip chart. I ask them to describe the pattern of the conversation, and to note points of agreement, as well as those that appear contradictory.

This recollection with reflection enables the conversation to go deeper in the next stage.

I resist giving my point of view on matters concerning the group because the purpose of the meeting is to enable the participants to understand each other to arrive at a meeting of *their* minds. Sometimes I am asked for my opinion, especially when there is a disagreement. I withhold my opinion; instead, I turn to the persons who seem to be in disagreement and ask them to explain *why* they think that way and *how* they came to that point, rather than explain the *what* of their position any further because I want people to understand each other better.

I have watched many teams of consultants stay awake an entire night before a big meeting with their client, preparing a huge 'deck' of slides to explain what they have learnt through their research and present a cogent solution. These consultants need a screen to show off their work. I have often come to meeting rooms with these consultants an hour before their big meeting. They check the position of the screen to see if it is visible from all the chairs around the room where the clients will be seated. They have already rehearsed which partner and which senior consultant will present which slides, while the juniors who did all the hard work to prepare the slides sit in some chairs behind—that is, if they are lucky to be invited to the meeting at all.

The junior consultants can crunch the numbers and ensure that they add up but they are unable to process the insights and emotions of their clients, or enable an alignment among them. The problem is, whatever synergies consultants compute with numbers will not be realized without an alignment of the aspirations of the leaders of a merged company, or any company for that matter.

That is why I wanted a flip chart and not a projection screen in the presidential suite of the Taj Mahal Hotel that morning.

REAL PEOPLE,
REAL PLACES, REAL THINGS

Be curious and listen to people, especially those who are not like you.

Young consultants have an impression that the senior partners of their companies always fly business class, entertain clients over expensive lunches, and present solutions to them in big boardrooms, supported of course by the sleek slides and graphs that were prepared by the young consultants.

Soon after I had joined ADL as a senior 'lateral' hire, brought into the firm at a higher level above the young consultants, I went on a long road trip in the USA. I drove myself in a rented car, stayed in motels in small towns, and drank coffee in plastic cups with truck dealers.

Sumant Moolgaokar, the chairman of TELCO had instructed me to walk around the factory and talk to workers if I wanted to learn what was really going on because statistical reports cannot reveal the whole truth. 'Rub your nose on the shop floor,' he had advised me. The Honda Motor Company, with which TELCO had a joint venture briefly, insisted its managers must 'see the real thing, in the real place, and meet the real people' before they presented any solution to the board. Therefore, checking it out for myself in order to learn had got into my bones.

My years of experience with TELCO, working in its factories in India producing trucks and buses, and setting up sales networks in other countries, had qualified me to join ADL's automobile consulting group. Japanese and European automobile companies were swarming over the US market at that time. US management consulting companies were busy, either supporting foreign companies to establish their businesses in the US, or in helping US companies to improve their operations and defend their market.

The world's largest truck makers, Mercedes-Benz Germany (TELCO's partner when the Tata Group entered the business of commercial vehicles in India), and IVECO, the commercial vehicle arm of the Italian Fiat group, wanted to break into the US truck market. They were wary though because the US truck industry was quite unlike the passenger car industry.

Whereas the cars sold in the US, like cars sold all over the world, are produced in large volumes in large factories and, similarly, trucks sold in the rest of the world are produced in large volumes in large factories, the trucks sold in the US are not. US truck buyers want their trucks custom-built to suit their personal requirements. Engines, transmissions and axles of trucks are produced by large manufacturers who specialize in designing and producing such precision-engineered components. Customers tell their truck dealer the combination of components they want and the truck company procures and assembles them. It ensures they fit together and guarantees that the package will work reliably and safely for the long distances across the US highways over which the drivers haul their loads. The cabins in which the drivers ride for many days and nights are, similarly, custom built to suit the driver's tastes.

Mercedes-Benz had presumed that the US truck market was ripe for well-engineered German trucks in which all the important components, such as engines, transmissions and axles are designed and made by Mercedes-Benz. Moreover, the costs of the trucks would be lower if standard Mercedes components were imported from large Mercedes factories—such as engines from the factory in Brazil. However, this impressive solution did not work. While US customers loved Mercedes' well-engineered cars and paid a lot of money for them, they were not willing to buy Mercedes' equally well-engineered trucks even if they were less expensive than the US-made trucks. Mercedes' venture failed and the company had to change its strategy. Instead, much later, it acquired Freightliner, a US truck manufacturer, and joined the US game of assembling trucks to US customers' requirements even if they did not prefer Mercedes components.

ADL was hired by IVECO to help it understand why the US customers would not buy well-engineered products at lower cost, as truck owners did in the rest of the world. IVECO's management wanted to understand the dynamics of truck demand and use more carefully before determining their strategy. Since I was a truck man, ADL gave me the assignment.

I decided I must analyse things for myself. Truck dealers are the connectors in the system; they know their customers and know the manufacturers' capabilities too. They can give valuable insights to manufacturers if they are willing to listen to them. (In fact, it was the insights from truck and bus dealers in Malaysia that enabled Tata Industries—TELCO's joint venture in Malaysia, which I had managed—to devise an innovative sales-and-service strategy by which it was able to sell more Tata trucks and buses within two years than Mercedes-Benz, the market leader in Malaysia at that time.)

I met dozens of truck dealers around the country. They explained to me how their businesses worked. Some introduced me to their customers, who discussed how *their* businesses worked and what their preferences were. Going out in the field to view things as they really are, rather than imagining what they might be when seen through spreadsheets of numbers, and listening to real people speak, enabled me to understand not only why the truck industry worked in the way it did in the USA, but also why it *must*, to fit into the system of the society and economy that has evolved in the country.

The cultures of countries and the business practices differ from one country to another because people do things differently and have good reasons for it. Companies also have strong cultures which can be sources of their competitive advantage. For example, the consistent high quality of some companies' products is a result of a culture of excellence the companies have created with persistence over decades. Just as social cultures are hard to change, a company's culture can be hard to change too. A company that wants to succeed in a new market may have to adjust its own culture to suit the market. If it is unable or unwilling to do so it would be best for the company to stay out of that market.

When I returned to India to consult with BCG in 2000, many foreign companies were feeling their way into India. They were attracted by the growth rate of the economy, the size of the middle class, and the low levels of consumption of many goods compared to levels in developed countries. Many presumed Indian customers would accept their products just as well as customers in other markets had. Only those who adapted their business models to fit India—rather than expecting India to change to accommodate them—succeeded. Those who could not change failed. They complained that their consultants had let them down. The consultants had presented graphs of economic trends and charts of sizes of customer segments but where they failed was they could not help the companies change their cultures to succeed in a new market.

Along with my colleagues from ADL, I explained to IVECO's executives what I had learnt about the US market, and also suggested to them they would have to change their mindset and methods of operation if they wanted to succeed there. They decided that a change would not be feasible. If they had ventured into the US market, ADL would have been assured of a very large consulting contract to assist them. Our honest recommendation lost us a lot of consulting revenues.

There are four lessons for consultants in this story:

First, consultants should not limit their explanations of market realities to quantitative data. Expert consultants listen attentively to diverse people and provide valuable insights to their clients into how complex socio-economic systems actually work.

Second, the consultant must have only the client's interest in mind. He should not seek any benefit from the client's decisions—neither financially, nor even to obtain credit for the client's success.

The third lesson is, enjoy learning. Consulting gives more opportunities to learn than working with one company for a long time can give because a consultant will serve many clients over time. Each new client and each new situation provides opportunities to meet diverse people and, by listening to their perspectives, to learn something new.

The fourth: Good consultants are good with numbers; very good consultants are very good listeners.

ALL FOR ONE AND NONE FOR ALL

Systems thinking and collaboration, even amongst competitors, are essential for solving complex problems.

Partners of consulting companies need training too. They must improve their capabilities to sell consulting services and to organize the delivery of consulting services.

Thirty partners and senior consultants of an international management consultancy assembled for a leadership training programme in a forest resort in Southern Germany. Their trainer was a retired officer of the United Kingdom Special Forces. They were intrigued about what he would teach them. They associated the British special services with James Bond, the man the British government would parachute behind enemy lines to bring down evil empires single-handedly. They expected to have some fun. Besides, a weekend in a resort in the lower Alps, was an appropriate setting for a party with good food and wine for potential James Bonds.

The trainer disabused them. He said training for Special Forces officers is very rigorous, comprising risky missions with limited resources. He evoked images of tough men in camouflage swinging through trees, not men in tuxedos drinking martinis—'shaken, not stirred' of course like James Bond's perfect martini.

He briefed them about their mission. They had been commissioned to improve a town in Europe. Their client was the mayor. Citizens were complaining about the crumbling infrastructure and poor quality of public services. Traffic was snarling. Public transport could not cope. Old infrastructure was causing the quality of water and sanitation services to deteriorate. Citizens were unhappy with education, health, and recreation services. He must make many improvements rapidly or he would not get elected again in four years' time.

Fortunately, relevant surveys had already been made about the condition of the various services. In fact, he had used these surveys in his own election campaign to unseat the incumbent mayor. His election promise was that he would fix the problems. Now he must deliver. It was a do-or-die mission for him.

The trainer split up the group of thirty into five teams of six each. Each team was assigned a problem and handed a dossier of information on it. There was a team for transportation, for water and sanitation, health services and for education and recreation. The fifth team was assigned the task of improving the planning of the city, the weak link in the system which was the root cause of all-round deterioration. This team had the chunkiest file of information.

The trainer briefly ran us through the plan for the day. He expected the team members to mingle amongst themselves, go through the information in their files and plan their work. The entire resort had been booked for the meeting, so they could meet anywhere they wanted to, in the building or in the grounds. However, coffee and tea were available only outside the main conference room. There was an old photocopier in the basement in case they wanted to make copies of the documents. Mobile signals were good on the premises and they could research online for any other information they wanted. Lunch would be served at 12.30 p.m. in the dining room. They would have to reassemble at 3 p.m. in the conference room for presentations by all the teams. 'Get on with it,' he said, 'the clock is ticking.' He hinted that there might be a prize for the best team.

The 'special forces' training was the agenda only for the first day of the weekend training programme. A colleague from Germany and I were responsible for the entire programme. When the teams left the room to accomplish their mission, the trainer and I picked up cups of tea and wandered outside to have a chat. He told me his fascinating story about the work he had done in the special services and how he had become a trainer of leaders in the corporate sector.

His training programmes were designed to make leaders aware that they cannot accomplish difficult missions alone. They need to look at situations from different perspectives to understand what is afoot. When they understand the underlying causes of issues, they will find the leverage points for action. Direct and often simple actions at critical junctures can produce the desired results. Therefore, they may not need many resources for complex missions. They need systems thinking to understand the whole situation and find partners for the resources they need. James Bond does find attractive accomplices, he joked!

He suggested that I might like to wander around and observe the teams at work, unless I had other urgent work of my own. It was a nice day and I chose to look around.

The teams rushed to the printer in the basement to make copies of their briefs for all members to study. The printer was slow; the briefs copious. I noticed that one group had settled down in the veranda at the head of the staircase to the printer room waiting for their turn. It had the largest document to copy. It was the team responsible for the overall plan. They became impatient. They split the big document into many parts for the team members to read individually.

Then there was competition to find the best places in the gardens. In an hour all the teams were busy, heads put together in animated discussions. The spirit of competition had been stirred. They came to lunch, jesting about who would come up with the best solution.

At 3 p.m. the group reassembled. Some had prepared sleek slide presentations, so a projector and a screen had been set up. They were professional consultants and knew how to make compelling pitches. When they were done, they waited anxiously for the trainer to declare the prize-winner. They were shocked when he said that they had failed the citizens of the city, and that they had guaranteed that their client, the mayor, would lose the election!

He pointed out that the plan for urban mobility, which was the sleekest of all the plans, and the one that would be completed fastest too, would probably cause the most damage to the city. The plan presented an exciting solution for urban mobility but disregarded its impact on the city's sewage and drainage systems and on the environment. He asked the team to put the proposed urban mobility plan alongside the proposed plans for sewage, drainage, parks and recreation. The obstacles the urban mobility plan would create for other plans became apparent.

'None of you examined how your solutions must fit with others,' he remarked. 'You were all busy working within your competing silos. None of you engaged in any intermediary meetings with other teams to adjust your plans. You did not spend any time together in the beginning, as you should have, to understand how the pieces may connect with each other. You did not build into your planning process any requirement for consultation amongst the teams. What about the team that was preparing the overall plan? None of the teams sat with it to see how your plans fit with the master plan. In fact, you were happy to beat that team to the copier, whereas they should have been the first to have access to it because they needed to grasp the whole picture to be able to guide you.'

The metaphor of 'redesigning an aeroplane while flying' makes very vivid what the consequences of applying a non-systemic approach to improving a complex system can be. If the team redesigning the wings were to put new wings on the plane before the teams that were redesigning the tail section and the nose had completed their work, the plane would crash.

A systems picture of the issues to be addressed, explaining the relationships amongst them, is hardly ever prepared to understand what issues must be clubbed together, he explained. Instead what is offered is lists of important issues with goals for each of them. Even if there was any systems thinking and analysis done to produce the list, it is lost. Thereafter teams and experts work hard, like the consultants in the training programme, to address their favourite causes. They may achieve their own goals but they will not make the whole system better unless they apply more systems thinking.

Deeply embedded 'theories-in-use' of how large, complex problems should be solved are not systemic in their approach, he pointed out. Governments, large corporations and even large developmental organizations, like the UN, do not work systemically. The UN is divided into many agencies who compete with each other for turf and budgets rather than collaborating with each other.

The lesson for the consultants was that they must learn systems thinking and learn to collaborate with each other if they want to help clients, in governments and corporations, to solve complex, systemic problems.

LOOKING OUT OF THE BOX

Management consultants must have their feet on the ground in the world of action, and at the same time, their heads in the clouds in the world of knowledge, to help their clients find innovative solutions to their tough problems.

Management consultants have to increase trade between two worlds rich with knowledge. On one side is the world of business and action where their clients must produce the outcomes they want in a world in which there is great competition and which keeps changing frequently. They have to find new ways to compete. When they do and succeed they change the world for everyone. Amazon and Facebook had started small. They began with innovative, out-of-the-box ideas. As they grew, they changed the rules of the game. Now others must follow suit and change or they will perish. The incumbents fear new innovators. Thus the game of life—a dynamic dance of innovation and competition, birth and extinction—carries on in the world of business.

On the other side of business is the world of research and knowledge where academicians search for explanations of why the world works in the ways it does. Management consultants can be good connectors of the worlds of ideas and action. In fact, ADL, the world's oldest management consulting company, was founded in 1886 by scientists in MIT to translate technical solutions found in MIT's labs into ideas for businesses. ADL was the company I had joined in 1989 when I moved from the world of industry in India to the world of consultants in the USA.

ADL was a unique consulting company in many ways. It had several research labs on its premises in Acorn Park in Cambridge, Massachusetts, where it also had a formal School of Management for senior executives from governments and industries from developing countries. The ADL School of Management was connected to networks of other management schools. One of these networks, the International Consortium of Executive Development Research (ICEDR), comprised professors who, periodically, conducted surveys of the new challenges that business leaders were facing around the world so that they could direct the research in their own universities to find useful solutions.

In 1997, ICEDR conducted a joint survey with ADL School of Management. The respondents were 2700 senior executives in twenty-eight global corporations with headquarters in North America, Europe, Asia and Australia.

The principal strategic challenge for global companies, the survey revealed, was the reconciliation of seemingly conflicting goals:

- Thinking long-term while delivering short-term results
- Developing global scale while being locally responsive
- Standardizing products and processes to increase efficiency, and also customizing products and services for every customer
- Investing in innovation while reducing costs and increasing operational efficiency
- Encouraging collaboration within the company and with partners outside while also building the competitive spirit within and also competing with others

In each aspect of this challenge—long-term vs short-term results, global vs local focus, innovation vs efficiency, collaborating vs competing—there is a tension between two necessary but apparently opposing goals, which need resolution. The companies seemed to be looking for a 'Yogi Berra solution'.

Yogi Berra, the famous baseball player, was known for his enigmatic one-liners of advice for managers. One was, 'If you don't know where you are going, you will end up somewhere else.' Another was, 'When you come to a fork in the road, take it!'

Business leaders seemed to be at a fork in the road. They needed to travel along both roads at the same time. How could they do this and yet be one organization?

A breakthrough solution to an 'either-or' dilemma is to convert it into a 'both-and' proposition by looking at

the issue in a different way. The academics realized that a
search for 'best practice' in business organizations would not
provide a solution because all the best businesses were facing
the same challenges. None had a solution. Therefore research
would have to be conducted outside the world of business
management.

Benchmarking

Consultants are often challenged by clients who ask
difficult questions. Their clients don't want theoretical
answers from them, but practical examples of what
will work for them. They want consultants who have
'domain knowledge' and understand their industries. The
consequence of this is that clients and consultants become
locked within the same box of ideas. Whereas, as the
academics in the ICEDR realized, the solution would have
to be found outside the box.

One of the global companies, a client of IA (the ADL
subsidiary I managed), which had participated in the survey,
had been keenly following developments in the field of
organizational learning at that time.

This company had been searching the business world for
a new form of organization suited to the rapidly emerging new
context. They had realized what should have been obvious at
the outset: there can be very few, if any, examples of this new
form, precisely because the old forms were appropriate for the
world in which businesses have operated so far. Furthermore,
business organizations and business schools have developed a

wealth of knowledge, concepts and tools for these older forms of organization, which have thus become widespread all over the world. Leaders of this company knew they had to find new principles for the twenty-first-century organization, as well as the tools and skills to create it, and it may be a while before they could hope to find many complete examples in the business world to 'benchmark'.

In fact, our client found a fertile field for benchmarking among living systems that seem to have resolved the problem of adaptation to highly interconnected and changeable conditions. Such systems, including biological and ecological ones, must efficiently adapt to their wider environment if they are to survive and grow. They have to keep innovating their forms, slowly or in spurts, as the environment around them changes. They also symbiotically use resources from the environment around them. Neural networks and some categories of computer programs that have these same characteristics of self-adaptation within a changing environment could also provide clues.

Our client realized that they would benefit from a surge in interest in the study of such self-adaptive systems by researchers in the field of complexity and also in the study of evolutionary biology. This was a field that I had been researching myself and I had written some papers about the application of principles of self-adaptive systems in the management of business organizations, which the client had read. I was invited to conduct a workshop within the client's company for a team of young leaders who were searching for organization design principles for resolving the management dilemmas they were facing. They wanted to know how they could implement Yogi Berra's enigmatic advice to 'take the fork in the road'.

Practical people are sceptical of ideas from other places and other fields. 'Very interesting,' they say, 'but it won't work here because we are different.' They are right. The idea must fit the situation in which it has to work. 'One size cannot fit all' is a realization that even the practitioners of public policy have realized because the contexts in which the solution must work can be very different, which is why practical people want customized solutions that fit their context.

Obviously, benchmarking with organizations similar to oneself is not helpful when one needs out-of-the-box solutions. On the other hand, solutions from outside the box may not be applicable at all. The way out of this dilemma is to first understand what is similar and what the fundamental differences are between one's own context and the other one which seems to provide interesting ideas.

Living Systems

My colleagues and I distinguished three types of systems of increasing complexity:

- Systems of mind, that is, systems of pure information, such as neural networks and computer programs
- Systems of mind and matter, such as biological systems

- Systems of mind, matter and spirit, which can only be human organizations, since human beings are the only living creatures known to have self-awareness and the desire and ability to consciously improve themselves

Ultimately, the new idea must fit into the basic structures of the organization that needs a new solution. As we conducted the research, we held the following four basic elements of a business organization as a conceptual framework:

- The way it chooses its direction and its strategies
- The way its organization is designed
- The way it manages its business processes
- The resources it deploys in its businesses

These four elements are the minimum critical set of elements of a business, government or a social-sector organization. Remove any one—strategy, organization, processes or resources—and the description will be incomplete. Many more features can be added. However, these are the four load-bearing pillars of an organization's architecture.

By looking at a broad array of living systems, an essential management principle is found for each of these four fundamental load-bearing pillars, which allows a business to have the capabilities it needs to convert its 'either-or' problems into 'both-and' solutions.

The four critical principles corresponding to the four fundamental elements of a high-performing business are:

- Strategy Formation: *Aligned Aspiration and Choice*
- Organization Design: *Permeable Boundaries*
- Process Management: *Minimal Critical Rules*
- Resources: *Flexible Architecture (requisite variety; adequate redundancy; latent potential)*

Our client had read my paper that enumerated these principles and was convinced they provided useful insights. However, he would have to convince others in his company too. The company had provided him with a team of fast-track leaders from different departments and a budget for research to come up with a working solution. He had a deadline too. The board wanted the team to present their solution early in the new year.

It was late October when my client approached me. There were less than three months to the deadline with the Christmas holidays in between. His team had already done some work with the assistance of other consultants. They were burrowing deeper 'within the box' and had made a list of interesting companies to benchmark that seemed to, more or less, have the qualities they were looking for. My client was fearful that if I presented nature as the system I had benchmarked for them, the team would think I was an alien from outer space.

He gave me the list of companies they had already shortlisted. He asked me to examine them and to be sure to include them as prime examples of the four principles, supplementing the list with other companies if I found it necessary.

I met his team in Houston just before the Christmas holidays. They had flown in from different parts of the USA; I came from Boston. Immediately after the meeting, everyone would be flying home to be with their families for the holidays; I would be going to India. The spirit of the meeting was both light, in anticipation of the holidays, as well as tense because their deadline had arrived and they had not yet found the breakthrough solution the board expected from them.

The meeting was successful. My client sent me a letter to thank me in the new year, with an extract from the team's report:

> From experts and others, whom we reference later in this chapter, we extracted a set of key learnings. Together they represent a good summary of our insights as they unfolded to us.

Disturbances in the system can be advantageous

We have been astounded at what happens when an apparent problem can turn into an opportunity. We had a profound learning from our experience with one of our consulting partners, Arthur D. Little. When another consulting firm was not able to respond to our request for help in the time frame that we needed, we turned to Arthur D. Little to help us with benchmarking, which they did very quickly.

> 'If we'd tried to set up plant visits for ten people, we'd still be doing it and wouldn't have half the content,' one team member reported. Further, it turned out that

one of Arthur D. Little's affiliate companies, Innovation Associates, housed expertise about the parallels and differences between biological living systems and human organizations and about systems thinking.

The four principles

Here is an explanation of the four principles that the team had learnt:

Permeable Boundaries: This principle of permeable boundaries suggests that a system that wishes to innovate and evolve must be engaged in an ongoing exchange with its environment. This principle is derived from a fascinating but fundamentally contradictory pair of ideas in physics and biology. On the one hand, the second law of thermodynamics, which governs our physical world, says that any isolated or closed physical system will proceed spontaneously to degenerate into disorder over time. On the other hand, biologists say that the living universe is evolving from disorder to order, towards forms of ever-increasing capability. So who is right? The physicists or the biologists? The answer: Both!

Biologists are describing open systems, in which any part that is evolving is connected with its environment and exchanges information and energy with it. Ilya Prigogine, who won the Nobel Prize in chemistry in 1977 for his work on the thermodynamics of non-equilibrium systems, extended this notion to the processes of self-organization and life. He showed how even purely physical systems, such as chemical solutions and streams of fluids, could self-organize into beautiful patterns if they continued to receive a flow of small inputs from their environment.

This principle of permeable boundaries applies to systems on any scale—individuals, species, complex ecosystems and even human societies. A species produces healthier variants through the exchange of genes among its members. Shut down these permeable boundaries and the system withers through in-breeding. Societies benefit from the market mechanism that enables trading of information and resources with others. Closed economies have always tended to decay.

Current examples of permeable boundaries in business abound. Most relevant are those instances in which organizations are trying consciously to break down the barriers that separate functions, product groups and businesses in order to stimulate sharing of best practices and innovation. In an effort to save precious weeks and months from their time-to-market (TTM), companies such as Hewlett-Packard, Honda, Johnson & Johnson, and Sony routinely assemble cross-functional teams with clear charters but small budgets—forcing them, in effect, to find ways to uncover and share resources that might otherwise have been 'owned' by one group or another. Other firms, such as Chrysler, have gotten exceedingly good at creating symbiotic relationships with their suppliers—to such an extent that vendors literally move into Chrysler factories for the life of their contracts. European companies such as Hoechst*, Philips and

---

* Hoechst AG [hø:kst]) was a German chemicals then life-sciences company that became Aventis Deutschland after its merger with France's Rhône-Poulenc S.A. in 1999.

Volkswagen have demonstrated great skill in using intellectual exchange with universities and technical institutes as a stimulus to their own product development and R&D efforts.

Minimal Critical Rules: The second principle is minimal critical rules. Systems that evolve to a higher order learn new and advanced rules, but for each rule they add they must shed an earlier rule. Christopher Langton, with the Santa Fe Institute (SFI), one of the principal centres for the study of complex self-adaptive organisms, experimented with computer programs such as the Game of Life and established that very few rules are required to produce complex, highly ordered behaviour. In fact, he found that if the number of rules was increased beyond the few vital ones, the system went into disorder rather than additional order. Stuart Kauffman and John Holland, also of the SFI, have confirmed this insight and extended it to the design of systems that learn new and better rules to make themselves more effective. Holland established the notion of an economy of rules, which is the foundation for what we refer to as minimal critical rules. If rules are not shed, the system will become less smart and less capable of further improvement. It is as if systems develop a 'Catch-22' situation when they have more rules, and the rules begin to contradict each other in an increasing number of situations.

When there are contradictions in the stated rules, people in societies and business organizations begin to ignore them and develop the so-called 'unwritten rules' to operate with. A problem with unwritten rules is that they cannot easily be examined, even by members of the organization themselves, and therefore cannot easily be altered. This inaccessibility of the rules impedes needed change and improvement of the system. So it seems desirable to have only a few important and explicitly understood rules, which are aligned with the organization's values and tacit norms.

Many executives and managers complain, often bitterly, about the excessive number of rules they create. Even when their goal is to standardize, 'commonize' or otherwise simplify their core processes, they find themselves awash in rules. However, a countercurrent can be found in a growing number of settings. For example, in Amoco Corporation a movement is under way to effectively manage business processes that cross-cut the company's product-based divisions. Stimulated by a desire to exploit the potential benefits of investments in enterprise-wide information management, Amoco came to recognize that it could realize those benefits only by replacing the complex thicket of measurements and reporting schemes required by the corporation with a limited number of big, clear, consistent rules on measurements and reporting.

Flexible Architecture: The principles of permeable boundaries and minimal critical rules apply both to systems of pure information and to biological systems. The third principle, flexible resources, applies to the design of matter itself in a way that enables species to evolve.

Stephen Jay Gould, the evolutionary biologist, describes this principle as 'flexibility in the component parts rather than their precise adaptation for their functions'. The principle manifests itself in three ways:

Latent potential, which enables innovations in function. Gould explains this with the '5-per cent-of-a-wing problem'. A row of feathers along the forearm cannot aid flight. So if wings were to evolve over generations, what would be the point of developing feathers before they became sufficient in size and number to aid flight? Why would the survival-of-the-fittest mechanism reward the incremental development of something that offered no apparent functional advantage? The answer is that feathers did not in fact evolve originally as a flight mechanism, and many feathered birds still do not fly. Feathers work superbly as thermoregulatory devices for conserving heat, and a bird can have many feathers to serve that purpose. However, as the species grew more feathers—for thermoregulation—they became sufficient at some point to enable a bird to take off when it flapped its forearms!

Redundancy, which enables additional or new functions. Suppose every gene an organism possesses is required for something vital to its life, then to make anything truly different, it would have to adapt one of its existing genes for a novel use. But then how would the organism perform its former necessary functions? In other words, the organism is stuck—optimally adapted to be sure, but in a permanent non-evolutionary rut. Therefore, all biological organisms (at all scales, from genes to organs) maintain massive redundancy—that is, a capacity for building more stuff or information than minimally needed to maintain a current adaptation. The 'extra' material then becomes available for constructing evolutionary novelties.

Requisite variety, which provides possibilities for innovations through new combinations. As we discussed earlier, the number of possible 'connections' influences the ability of a system to innovate through new combinations. If an organism does not have sufficient variety in its own resources, it must be part of a larger ecosystem that has the requisite variety, and it must have permeable boundaries with the larger system.

The principle of flexible resources (through latent potential, redundancy and requisite variety) is demonstrated in several organizations recognized in their industries for their innovativeness and flexibility. For example, personnel in 3M move back and forth between dual career paths, thereby increasing the variety in their skills and improving flexibility. Honda has built flexibility into its resource-allocation processes in many ways: the way it deploys people in project teams, the approach it has taken to designing the platform of its world car (Accord), and even the machinery and equipment it uses to manufacture automobiles.

Aligned Aspiration: Obviously, human systems are more complicated than other biological systems because human beings are the only known organisms that have self-awareness and egos. For example, human beings create identities for themselves over and above their physical identities and they work hard to preserve and enhance them. They create abstract visions, set goals and consciously choose strategies to accomplish their goals. Human beings and organizations seek to understand the conditions that will lead to their own improvement and further evolution—and so they deliberately create these conditions.

The principle of building and aligning aspirations of the members of an organization is very clearly seen in companies that are adaptive and agile. People are aligned towards the broad goals of the organization and they share values that they begin to cherish. A lot of changes and improvements are brought about by cross-boundary teams that set their own challenging goals, aligned with the broader goals of the firm. These goals act as magnets for the teams, drawing them together and onward. This contrasts with the 'push' approach, in which goals, mostly financial, are imposed down the chain of command and people do not feel drawn by the 'pull' of a challenging goal.

It is important to note that aligned aspirations, magnets and the like rarely come about as a result of top-down threats or 'burning platform' speeches. They may be precipitated by crisis, but their essential qualities of engagement, widespread commitment and durability come about through a process of shared visioning (as opposed to vision sharing). Hence, companies that realize their aspirations will not be achieved without significant shifts in culture, have committed to investing in long-term, broad-based employee involvement at all levels of the organization.

DROPPING A BOMB

Change-makers should understand the combination of forces shaping the system they want to change before they implement their solutions, or else their fixes could backfire.

Peter Senge's *The Fifth Discipline: The Art and Practice of the Learning Organization* became a bestseller when it was published in 1990. The CEOs of companies proudly displayed it in their offices. But very few actually read it. In fact, the book was described by one reviewer as the most published and least read management book at that time!

As its title suggests, the book advocates five disciplines that must be learnt and applied by those who want to make a positive change in the world. The disciplines range from personal mastery on one side to systems thinking on the other with team learning included in the spectrum. Personal mastery (with the segment of shared vision adjacent to it) focuses on the understanding and strengthening of a leader's own strengths and value systems. Systems thinking (with mental models as an adjoining concept) focuses outwards to understand the interplay of forces causing the events and trends we observe in the world around us, and the lenses (mental models) through which we see them. Team learning sits in the middle of the book's content. It looks at ways in which people bring their personal masteries and visions together to make changes in the world. People form teams on many scales—small project teams, large organizations and even nations—to pool their energies together and produce the desired outcomes.

Charlie Kieffer and Peter Senge's consulting company, Innovation Associates, provided training programmes and consultancy services in each of the five disciplines. The personal mastery programmes were influenced, to a great extent, by the eastern traditions of meditative practice and inward reflection in which Peter Senge had great interest as he had travelled to India to learn from the Brahmakumaris, and to China to learn from Buddhist masters. The systems thinking programmes had their roots in the scientific departments of MIT, in the studies of systems dynamics. Michael Goodman and Jennifer Kemeny (and Senge himself), who were the core of IA's systems thinking practice, were graduates of MIT.

The most popular programmes were those on personal mastery and systems thinking. As the company's business grew, the number of trainers specializing in the disciplines grew too. The 'personal masters' said the 'systems thinkers' were too dry and objective, and the 'systems thinkers' ribbed the 'personal masters' that they were too sentimental and squishy.

I was a consultant with IA and not a trainer, having joined the company when ADL, where I was consulting, acquired IA.

I was trained in its consulting process Visionary Leadership and Planning (VLP), which IA had developed combining all the disciplines. Within the disciplines, I focused on systems thinking because it was most useful for my consulting work in business strategy. Systems thinking enables clients to visualize scenarios of the future formed by changing shapes of industries, economies and societies. Thus, they can sense emerging opportunities for growth of their businesses, which they would not be able to with extrapolations of prevalent trends.

'Scenario planning', founded on systems thinking, was formulated into a process for developing business strategy by the Royal Dutch Shell oil company in the 1980s. Peter Schwartz, the head of Shell's strategy team, wrote a path-breaking book on scenario planning, *The Art of the Long View,* in 1991. Kees van der Heijden, who later led Shell's team, wrote another book, *Scenarios: The Art of Strategic Conversation.* Upon leaving Shell, Peter founded a strategic consulting company in California in the mid-1990s, the Global Business Network (GBN)*, and Kees had joined him. I had read both their books, and I'd been following the development of scenario planning with great interest.

With their common interest in systems thinking, IA and GBN ran a master class in scenario planning in IA's offices in Waltham in 1998. Kees had designed the class. He selected four persons from GBN's network of clients and practitioners, who had recently used scenario planning in

---

* Defunct since 2013; acquired by Deloitte

strategy consulting work, to present. I was the fifth presenter, recommended by IA to the master class, to share what I had learnt while assisting my Indian client, the Bharat Petroleum Corporation Limited (BPCL), to apply systems thinking and scenario planning in its programme of transformation. Not only was I the sole presenter from IA, but also the only non-westerner making a presentation, and my case was the only one from outside the western world. Naturally, there was curiosity about what I had to offer.

I was also the last presenter. The insightful presentations by the other four were greatly appreciated, especially the discussions that followed each one to distil the essence of the practice of scenario planning.

I had assisted my client, BPCL, to apply the VLP process, which includes all the five disciplines. They had begun the process of scenario planning after they had gone through some steps of personal mastery and, especially, shared vision. (I have narrated how they released the power of shared vision in the story, *The Harley Test*.) They expressed their compassion for the poor people in the country and their commitment to make BPCL the most trusted petroleum company in the country. They looked at the world around them through the lens of this vision. Therefore, the scenarios they prepared contained not only economic forces, which scenarios prepared by business corporations mostly do, but included the social conditions of the country too. These scenarios seemed richer and more insightful, though simpler in their expressions, than the scenarios that the presenters before me had shared. The participants of the master class seemed to be resonating the most with what I was sharing.

I had barely finished, when an earlier presenter, whose scenarios were technically the best and who had been glowing in the accolades, made a sarcastic remark about my country.

A few months before, the Indian government had tested a nuclear device in Pokhran, in the Rajasthan desert. There was great consternation around the world about India acquiring a nuclear weapon which India's neighbours, Pakistan and China, already had. India felt that it should have its own defensive capability as a deterrent to trouble from its neighbours. However, countries that already had nuclear bombs, such as the US, were alarmed at the proliferation of nuclear technology.

This presenter was from the US. He commented that the Indian government was wasting money on nuclear weapons when there were so many poor people in the country. He may have been right so far, perhaps, but it is what he said next which provoked me. He said, 'We cannot trust less civilized countries with dangerous weapons.'

In a flash I retorted, 'The only country that has ever dropped a nuclear bomb on a civilian population is . . .'

I did not have to complete my sentence. The Europeans in the room were smirking and my challenger became very angry. Jenny Kemeny intervened immediately. 'Time for our coffee break,' she said, and pulled me outside.

Jenny then popped a question to me which changed my life. 'You clearly love your country so much. Why are you wasting your talents in helping rich western companies make more money? Why don't you give more of your life and talents to helping India?'

I changed course. My wife, Shama, and I decided we would return to India. Our children had completed their education and had set out well in their own lives. Nothing stood in the way. I wrote to Montek Ahluwalia, who was then a member of the Planning Commission of India, and offered to introduce the process of scenario planning to him. On my return from the US, I helped the Confederation of Indian Industry (CII) and Montek to undertake an experimental application of the process within the breadth of India's complexities.

WANTED: NEW SOLUTIONS

Good consultants enable their clients—companies and even countries—to learn to find and implement their own solutions.

India is a large country with a lot of diversity. There are many divisions within the nation: many political parties, regions, religions, economic strata, etc. What binds it all is a democratic process that requires different interests to be considered. However, the way democracy is playing out in India is messy with the various groups acting blatantly in their self-interest. The parliamentary process, by which the many interests have to be finally reconciled, seems now to be anything but a good and reasonable process in the country. Often it is chaotic.

Sometimes the opportunity that is manifest in India— its billion-plus people and its system of democratic government—seems to be its very problem! A population of a billion-plus human beings can be an attractive market for businesses and a large source of workers, but presently the size of the population is perceived as a burden to policymakers.

Although democracy gives the people a voice, it makes it very difficult for them to take fast, aligned action.

Traditional governance methods and models seem to have not worked well in India to produce an all-round inclusive and sustainable growth. It is obvious that the country needs a new solution—a sustainable, deep-reaching solution—to accelerate socio-economic development. India may be the ultimate proving ground for any new approach to management and governance. Marked by deep structural imbalances, the country is unrivalled in its complexities. There is far more diversity in the Indian social and political make-up than in any other country. If an approach to democratically accelerate socio-economic development can be made to work in India, chances are it can be made to work anywhere in the world.

So far Indians have believed that since resources—of money and managerial manpower—are scarce, they must not only plan carefully but also centrally monitor and control how these resources are used. The worst consequence of this is not the wastage of resources through inept, and often corrupt, planning and implementation, rather it is the almost helpless dependence of the people on the government to provide society with the very basics of civility—clean surroundings, discipline and respect for each other's needs, as well as its almost total dependence on government's strained and leaky apparatus to provide other basic necessities, such as water, healthcare and education.

Many complex, systemic problems have to be resolved to accelerate the desired change in India: the inadequacy of the education system, the poor quality of the physical infrastructure, chronic and deteriorating power and water supply, and the list goes on. To find solutions to such complex problems require many people from different institutions, and with different perspectives, to work together.

Fortunately, several individuals and organizations are stepping forward to share the responsibility of development of the country. They are concerned about the situation. They realize that they cannot just sit around waiting for the government to push growth into high gear. That may take forever. But unfortunately, even though individually they possess the capability to address parts of the complex problems, they are not able to work together effectively to find comprehensive solutions to rectify the situation.

All these concerned parties—NGOs, citizens, political parties, motivated government officials, industry—have diverse perceptions and diverse agendas, and therefore find it impossible to pull together in one direction. Each of them feels that it has the sure medication that is required to cure the ills plaguing India. But are these medicines suitable? Are they tried and tested? And, who is willing to accept the prescription recommended by individual experts?

Clearly what ails India and what the country's future direction should be needs deep thinking and understanding of diverse situations before any prescription can (or indeed should) be suggested. But the various participants in the system are somehow not able to engage in a meaningful dialogue that will allow them to align their thoughts and actions.

Of course, there exist many forums for discussion and debate among the many groups who must be consulted before any action can be undertaken, following the format of the parliamentary process, as mentioned earlier. There are also many formal and informal meetings outside the parliamentary process, such as meetings sponsored by industry associations between business people and government.

These meetings, which often also include people from outside India, brim over with information, advice, examples and solutions. But since all stakeholders are unable to forge an alignment, the outcome following these meetings is unproductive resulting in unprofitability and frustration.

The frustration is not restricted to only those who participate in the meetings. Rather, it is a phenomenon that builds up across the country. Some constituents of the Indian system of stakeholders and institutions express their frustration through unilateral, self-serving and often violent behaviour. Many others become passive. While several others resort to finding 'special', even unethical, ways to work through the slow and inept system to aggrandize themselves. Thus they corrupt an already overstrained system, rendering it even less capable of serving society's needs efficiently. All these behaviours are draining positive energy from the system and leading slowly but surely to its disintegration.

Frustration sometimes reaches a point where the Indian people, citizens of a democracy, express a yearning for a strong central authority to 'clean up' the country. They cite examples: 'See how well things are going in China!' or 'Look how Singapore has progressed since its independence.'

These people point to the benefits of a strong central authority for the economic progress of these countries. It's a dangerous yearning, but they are conditioned to the concept of central authority. Faced with a situation where the democratic government doesn't seem to yield the desired results and where they themselves feel too powerless to do anything, they often catch themselves wishing for the advent of an authoritarian central power, a 'benevolent dictator' perhaps, who can fix it all.

The acceleration of change in the country requires aligned action by many groups across the country: civic society, government, business and political parties. Since this coordination does not exist, India finds itself hamstrung. What is the way out? Not more detailed plans, nor more expert advice, but a solution to address the root cause itself—the people's inability to act in alignment with each other to benefit the whole country. If a solution can be found to this root problem in India's progress, positive change can be accelerated and new confidence created among citizens. The need for working outside the system to satisfy one's own needs and the desperate yearning for a central authority will abate.

What I have described above seems like India in 2020, but actually it was a description of India in 1998. (India's economy has grown since then, but problems of inequity and environmental degradation persist, in fact, India's pattern of growth has worsened them.)

I shared this analysis with two friends in India in November 1998. One was Montek Singh Ahluwalia. Montek had been a leader of the reform of the Indian economy in the early 1990s that was spearheaded by Dr Manmohan Singh, minister of finance in the cabinet of Prime Minister Narasimha Rao. Montek was Secretary in the ministry of finance at the time. His clear thinking and drive had made a vital contribution to the process of reform. By 1999, as governments changed, and new political parties came to power, Montek found himself in the Planning Commission of India. The Planning Commission was a hangover from an era gone by—the era of centralized planning of the economy in the socialist style, (dare one say the Soviet style?) 'What was Montek's role in the Planning Commission?' I wondered. So I wrote to him offering him my analysis of the need for a new process for catalysing change in the country by creating further alignment among various sections of society. He was intrigued and we agreed to meet.

The other friend was Tarun Das, director general of CII. CII had been an important facilitator of the first generation of the economic reform process in the 1990s. In fact, Tarun and Montek were good friends. I felt that Tarun and CII may be in a position to facilitate a new conversation between a broader swathe in OED of society than the economists, civil servants and business people who had played a major role in the first generation of reforms in the 1990s.

Tarun, Montek and I examined the generative scenario thinking approach applied in South Africa in the early 1990s and the variants of this approach tried in other countries. Montek was most intrigued by the scenarios for Japan developed by GBN, an organization based in San Francisco that had worked with some Japanese business people to project plausible outcomes for different approaches to bring about reform, or lack thereof, in the Japanese financial and industrial system. What intrigued him was the way in which very complex economic conditions had been described so evocatively in the form of stories of people. He pointed to the piles of reports lying in his own room. 'I have dozens of people with PhDs in economics, including myself, churning out masses of tables and projections,' he said, 'but are we looking at the right things? And, what constructive effect do reports full of statistical data have, even if we are?'

The generative scenario thinking process

Generative scenario thinking has emerged from a combination of two disciplines of management. One is scenario planning that had originated after World War II as a tool for military strategy and was later adapted as a management technique by large private corporations, and the other is vision alignment, the essence of which is to align the aspirations of key players in a system.

Royal Dutch Shell and other corporations began to use the scenario planning methodology in the 1970s and '80s to understand the complex phenomena that impacted their business. For Shell, the price of oil is an important variable that can cause big swings in the company's performance. But the price of oil is pretty much beyond Shell's control as it is determined by the interplay of many variables—some political, some economic and some technological.

Scenario planning is fundamentally different from another approach that also uses the term 'scenarios'. In this latter approach, consultants and experts attempt to predict what the future will be. They often get it wrong. Hence this predictive approach to planning does not have much credibility. It is fundamentally flawed because it attempts to predict a future in complex conditions with many variables, where neither their interactions nor their future strengths are fully known. The practitioners of this predictive approach try to give a map of a territory into which none has ventured so far. Scenario planning, on the other hand, (continuing the metaphor of a journey into new territories) provides the people who have to venture forth with a compass. It points to the right direction of their desired destination. In addition, scenario planning suggests the early warning signs people should expect to see to confirm the way the future is unfolding.

The other discipline, vision alignment has been incubating in the processes of organizational learning, which are fast spreading across the world today. Traditional planning techniques are limited in their ability to factor in and manage the emotional needs of the principal actors in a system. In their drive for rationality and quantification they either totally ignore, or inadequately address the real and powerful emotional motivations of people. Techniques and tools for vision alignment enable groups of interacting players to include such 'softer' factors in the planning process in a deliberate and purposeful manner.

Using a combination of both these disciplines, the generative scenario thinking process enables the parties involved to focus on *what might happen* as well as on what each of them *would like to happen*. However, it is *not* a process of negotiation, wherein one must identify the positions and interests of the parties and find a way to narrow them down and reconcile them.

The distinguishing characteristic of the generative scenario thinking process is that it has been found to be very effective in creating deep conversations and learning among people who are a part of one large system, but who have tremendous competition among themselves and perhaps very different values. And who can, by acting in their own self-interest, inadvertently damage the whole of which they are a part.

Generative scenario thinking enables people to discover together the end result they all desire and to obtain the insights they need to focus on the critical principles and actions that will help them achieve the desired result. For example, the process was used in the early 1990s (prior to the abolition of the apartheid) in South Africa, when the differences between the various races and political parties could have blown the country apart.

Representatives of white and black parties, social workers and other community leaders adopted a variation of the process to strike up a dialogue between themselves and envisage a shared vision of the future for the country. Thirty-odd people from various sectors of society got together to imagine what South Africa could become if certain forces played out in certain ways. For example, what would happen if the black and white people refused to cooperate.

They developed four alternative scenarios for the future of South Africa. They shared these scenarios and their insights with the driving forces that could bring them about across the country. This in turn influenced the thinking of many people and contributed to South Africa's successful transition out of apartheid and on to the world's political and economic stage.

A few years later the process was used in Colombia where representatives of the military, government and civil society, as well as the guerrillas, came together to project alternative futures for Colombia, a country torn apart by conflict among these groups. Some of the guerrilla leaders participated in this process, called Destino Colombia, from their jail cells!

Generative scenario thinking saves participants from getting tangled in their differences. It focuses their attention on the domain they all have in common, which in the South African situation was the future of South Africa. The participants in the process did not have to agree, in the first stage of discussion, on a concrete solution to the country's problems. They only arrived at a consensus on some aspects of how the entire 'system' of South Africa actually worked, on the complex nature of the crisis, and on some possible outcomes of the current conditions. At the same time, the recognition of a shared aspiration for the future stability of South Africa greatly facilitated the processes of negotiation which also had to take place, since the 'system' included people with divergent interests.

What sets generative scenario thinking apart is the approach factors in the new variables of uncertainty and multiple stakeholders that define the world today and are especially magnified in complex systems such as the Indian state. Instead of trying to forecast the future, an exercise in futility, the methodology provides a framework for leaders to connect with other people, collect inputs from diverse individuals and use them to construct alternative scenarios of the future. This is very different from prediction.

There is no one forecast as such. Rather, organizations and nations equip themselves with an array of scenarios that they are likely to encounter in the future. While the most important certainties appear in all the scenarios, the most important uncertainties distinguish the different scenarios. People begin with a mass of information and end up with a set of easily communicable images.

The process urges people to think outside their usual mental boxes—to explore different logics, different viewpoints and different variables. They learn from each other, and a collective way of thinking emerges from this learning process. Then this collective thinking is used to construct alternative images of how the future might unfold.

Instead of relying on the old crutches of authority, generative scenario thinking advocates harnessing the power of aligned aspirations to try and arrive at the preferred scenario. Since leaders can no longer order implementation, they are forging tools and techniques to create a shared vision that will inspire people to rise above their differences and work together to achieve it.

The pioneering pathfinder of the approaches for generative scenario thinking is Adam Kahane. Adam had worked in Royal Dutch Shell's corporate scenario thinking team in the 1980s. He had facilitated the unusual experiment in the early 1990s in South Africa (described above) to use the principles and techniques of scenario planning. Thereafter, he has worked on scenario thinking processes in Canada, Guatemala, Colombia and other countries. Adam provided invaluable guidance to me in 1999 when I was assisting a group in India to develop scenarios for India.

The Indian experience

Tarun, Montek and I decided to invite twenty people to an informal meeting in January 1999. These persons, from heterogeneous fields—business people, civil servants, educationists, newspaper editors, social workers and lawyers—assembled to consider the generative scenario thinking process and its applicability to India. All of them, eminent in their own professions, were somewhat disillusioned with the traditional planning and implementation process. They were on the lookout for a course that would allow them and their fellow Indians to achieve three basic goals:

- Accelerate the pace of positive change for people in the lower half of the socio-economic pyramid
- Improve, greatly, the quality of civic life
- Improve the manageability and efficiency of the development process

Most of the persons came to the meeting with zero expectation. Sure, the invitation sounded intriguing, but they were all used to meetings that promised quick fixes to the Indian problem but fizzled into nothing.

However, their cynicism started evaporating soon. The more they heard about the process, the more it seemed suited to India. First, it was built to factor in diversity, the one characteristic about India that defeats the most comprehensive of strategies. Second, it relied on individuals, not governments: an important factor in a country where even though citizens stand disenchanted with the state, they feel too powerless to take any action themselves.

It seemed too much to hope that the few people who had gathered could change India by themselves, with anything less than a magic wand! What they collected from the generative scenario thinking process was not a magic wand but a different way of approaching large-scale change. They wondered if this was how they could begin to make a difference. They asked themselves, 'If not this, then what? If not now, then when? And if not us, then who?'

Once the applicability of the process was established, the group's next task was to identify a kernel of people who were committed to the Indian cause, were experts in their fields, and were willing to devote both time and mind to the process. These people would be perceived as sponsors within the system, facilitators who have viewpoints to contribute and the ability to draw others into action.

Each participant in the meeting submitted a list of eligible people. These individual lists were compiled, and from that thirty people were selected. Together the thirty constituted an assembly that enjoyed credibility, represented great influencing power and incorporated within itself several diverse ideological trends. These persons, including many from the original twenty, took up the baton to customize the processes of generative scenario thinking to Indian conditions and develop scenarios and insights for accelerating change in India.

Generative scenario thinking was used in India to focus primarily on two questions—'Whither India' and 'What are the drivers to accelerate the change we desire'. The process was intended to generate a long-term national agenda that could be shared with all sectors of society to catalyse the desired change in the country.

The process was anchored in three workshops held in New Delhi in 1999. CII provided the infrastructure to support the process. In the course of the three workshops, they involved over 100 people—experts in different fields, students, women from rural areas and even street children. These people from diverse backgrounds participated in the structured process to elicit and share aspirations, experiences and insights. Thus different perspectives were brought together.

At the outset the participants were acquainted with the generative scenario thinking process and the experience of its applicability to South Africa, Canada, Colombia and Japan, and then they were left to deliberate on ways in which the methodology could be made to work in India. After intense discussion that extended over three days, the participants ended the workshop by outlining a process to suit the Indian situation.

It was decided that if in South Africa the process was a square dance where firm steps were laid down and specific dancers identified, in India it would have to be more like a Garba, a folk dance, where people can keep joining and leaving. Even though efforts would be made to ensure that the core group remained more or less the same throughout the process, the procedures would be designed in such a way that the entry or exit of participants would not hamper it.

Also, equally important, the workshop laid down the five ground rules the participants would have to follow both in this and future sessions:

- Positive thinking
- Preparedness to think creatively—to move to a different paradigm
- Concentration on what I can do, rather than what others need to do
- Delivery against promise
- Ending with consensus

The first workshop was followed by two more three-day workshops, which involved over 100 people in the process—bureaucrats and activists, CEOs and rural women, education experts and street children, students and political heads. Although not all-inclusive, the selection of people was to a large extent representative of the various groups and views in the Indian society.

All persons stood on an equal footing with each other in the workshops; no one was talking down to anyone. Everyone presented their own points of view, which were followed by discussions. The viewpoints that came up repeatedly were embraced as the common points. Gradually, painstakingly, a shared language was created.

Establishing a dialogue between the participants was not simple. People had rigid mindsets, and breaking their preconceived notions was not easy. But two things helped. First, the scenario methodology promotes an informal, almost playful approach where everyone gets to say their piece and they are encouraged to say it not in the usual presentation style but in a direct, gripping fashion that helps both the speakers and listeners to focus, fast. For instance, in the very first workshop each participant was asked to bring an object which to them represented the current reality in India. Some dismissed the move as gimmickry. But when the others started using the objects to explain their perception of India, everyone realized the power of imagery that the process encouraged.

The second thing that helped was that the people at the workshops were there in their individual capacities, not as representatives of the groups they were identified with. This gave them the freedom to open their minds to other views, and even accept opinions that were contradictory to their interests but were in the country's interest.

Of course, there were arguments and clashes along the way, but since the participants had consciously agreed to accommodate differences in perception the group did not get polarized. With everyone focusing on the common points, disagreements did not flare into disputes. The desire to understand and include others ruled the entire process.

After an initial discussion, the issues included in the individual agendas were chalked up on the group agenda. These were examined and distilled and only the essentials were chosen as the final agenda. By this process of analysis, the group arrived at a consensus about the most important issues to address. They did not allow themselves to fall back on the agreement on the least controversial issues as an easy means to consensus.

Often, it was not easy for the participants to suspend their own mindsets, which had developed over the years. This posed a challenge for them as they had never participated in a process that required them to think together as intensively as the scenario process did. Slowly, painfully, they learnt to set their own beliefs aside and embark on the journey of collective thinking.

The scenario journey started with the participants sharing their views of the current reality in India. Then together they identified the areas of concern. Each workshop member was asked to identify the single most important thought or fear that as an Indian worried them about their country and the direction in which it was going. The concerns were collated and the themes that were recurring culled out. It was found that one emerging theme was the breakdown of moral and ethical values along with a passive acceptance of this breakdown. Other areas of concern that emerged related to education, governance, unemployment, poverty, women's position in India, environment, population, lack of rural empowerment, and communal and religious differences.

The members of the group divided themselves into subgroups and each took up one area of concern to explore further. CII provided the secretariat where the groups could deliberate and, when needed, experts from outside the group were involved in the process. Each subgroup was charged with the responsibility of producing backgrounders, facts, benchmarks, best practices, trends and exciting ideas tried elsewhere related to its area of concern. They met with experts, found reports that had been published, held mini seminars and brought back valuable insights and ideas. To the second workshop they invited people whom they felt the whole group could learn from. They were university professors, social workers, corporate leaders, students and even street children from New Delhi!

The second three-day-long workshop took place in a huge hall where the walls were covered from top to bottom with plain white paper. As the workshop progressed, people covered the walls with notes and pictures of the insights they were obtaining. Soon patterns began to emerge. The group sat back and reflected on these patterns and from that emerged insights into the leverage points in the complex system. Thus, the group had progressed from the symptoms and worries they had listed in the first workshop, to causes and to a few points of action that could alter the system favourably. These actions appeared to be the fundamental driving forces to produce the desired outcomes. (These driving forces are presented in the next chapter.)

The group then sat and looked at the patterns on the walls again. Four alternative scenarios for the future of India were hazily visible. It seemed that if the driving forces played out in different ways, these alternative scenarios may come about. It was like a kaleidoscope. The driving forces were the axis around which the system, that is, the whole country, could turn. And depending on which way it turned, the many pieces would assemble into four different patterns.

The majority wanted to describe the scenarios in the form of stories of the lives of poor people in the rural areas because they felt the masses could then relate more easily to what was being said. So the stories were written and shared in a third workshop. Some media and communication experts were also invited. The workshop was divided in its views on the best medium of expression, and the majority felt that the narrative stories with real characters were the best. Such stories, developed by GBN along with some Japanese industrialists, had been the medium for expressing the future of Japan.

However, others felt that metaphors and visual images would be far more effective in conveying the message as people would be able to translate these to their own situations, whereas in the stories people may not be able to relate themselves to the real characters. Or, if they could, they may get mired in the details of the stories.

The group decided to carry out some trials. The four scenarios were translated into stories as well as simple metaphors and pictures. The stories were tried with a few small audiences and the pictures with others. The latter turned out to be far more effective, proving once again that one picture can be worth a thousand words. (The images that emerged from the trials are described in another story to follow—The Doughnut Not the Hole.)

Many people who were directly involved with the generative scenario thinking process or who participated in the dissemination later have talked about the effect of the process on their attitude and actions. Some said that their hopes were kindled when they saw the way forward. Others were galvanized to take action guided by the insights. They said they could see the 'difference with which they could make the difference'.

Generating hope, insight and commitment among an increasing circle of people from diverse walks of life may be the greatest benefit of the approach.

REDESIGNING THE
AEROPLANE WHILE FLYING

The best consultants are lifelong learners, searching for better ways to make the world better for everyone.

Scenario planning for developing strategies for a country is more difficult, by an order of magnitude, than creating scenarios for a company. After Jennifer Kemeny put the thought into my head (in the master class in Waltham) that I should consider working in India, and when Montek Ahluwalia accepted my proposition to apply scenario planning to the future of India, I asked Kees van der Heijden, the master of the master class, for guidance.

According to Kees, Adam Kahane, to whom he introduced me, was the only person who had used systems thinking based scenario planning until then at a country level. The evocative scenarios which the process produced for South Africa's future were called the Mont Fleur scenarios, named after a country hotel in which the participants had met for several workshops over many months. Adam has given an account of the process in his book, *Transformative Scenario Planning: Working Together to Change the Future* (San Francisco: Berrett-Koehler, 2012).

Since his work in South Africa, Adam had applied his methodology, generative scenario planning, in other countries. Generative scenario planning begins with an alignment of participants' visions, just like I had done with my version of scenario planning in BPCL. Adam had also applied scenario planning methods in Japan and Canada, albeit on a broad policy area only, such as education, and not on the future of a country. He was very excited at the possibility of adapting what he had learnt in South Africa to India, a much larger and more complex country. However, he could not come to India as he was already committed to work in a South American country. He offered to teach me whatever he had learnt and encouraged me to set out on my adventure in India.

Adam invited me to his home in Boston where he explained to me what he had done in South Africa. He generously gave me a document he had prepared describing the methodology. His process was anchored in three, three-day-long workshops, many weeks apart, with research and consultations in between. Adam insisted that all the participants must attend all three workshops. I explained to him that this was not possible in India. Most people were unwilling to make firm commitments far ahead. Even if they did, they were likely to call the day before, or even just before a meeting (if they were 'very important' people) to say they could not come or offer to 'drop in' for a little while. The same thirty participants, for three days, three times, over nine months! That did not sound like India to me, I told him. I said I would have to adapt the process to fit Indian realities.

I offered an analogy—that of jazz. Musicians in a jazz combo coordinate without a complete musical score, unlike a symphony orchestra, where the conductor and all the musicians have a detailed score to guide them. Adam is Canadian, so to fit my analogy I described to him my lovely musical experience in the public square in Quebec City.

My wife Shama, our children and I were visiting as tourists. An accordionist was playing in the square. A young woman with a backpack was passing by. She was moved to dance a bit. She put down her backpack, danced a few steps to the delight of the accordionist, and dropped some coins into his cup. A couple who had been watching decided to join in. They began to dance. The girl went away, but they carried on the dance. Some others joined in. Soon a crowd was dancing, all to the same rhythm. The girl had gone, and the first couple to dance had gone too, but the dance continued—different dancers but the same dance, which continued at least for the half hour we were there. (For the record, my daughter, who loves to dance, and I danced too).

What will work in India, I said, is a process with a rhythm, but without a detailed score specifying what must be done when. Adam was intrigued. We discussed what would be the 'minimal critical requirements' to make the process work. With his assurance that he would continue to coach me, I set out. The 'systems dance'—a less regimented version

of the scenario planning process—worked quite well in India,
as explained in the story 'Wanted: New Solutions'.

Going down and up the U

Three years later Adam gave me a pleasant surprise. He said
he would be spending a lot of time in India over the next
few years, to apply another powerful consulting process to
one of India's most challenging problems, viz. persistent
malnourishment of India's children. Levels of malnourishment
were higher in India than that of the much poorer countries
in sub-Saharan Africa, despite the fact that India's economy
was more developed, it has some of the finest medical experts
and economists in the world, and it has one of the world's
largest government programmes for solving this problem
with a budget of over $1 billion a year.

Adam had become the managing partner of an innovative
consulting company. This new company had developed a
process, which they called the 'U-process'. It applied methods
that were developed by two remarkable persons—Joseph
Jaworski (author of the book *Presence*) and Otto Scharmer
(author of *Theory U: Leading from the Future as It Emerges*).
Their process combines three movements represented in the
shape of a U.

The first movement, descending the left side of the U, was
called 'sensing': developing a felt sense of the current reality
of the system that one is trying to understand and change.
This is a process of listening deeply to the stakeholders of
the system, whose actions, or lack of actions, are creating the

conditions that one wants to change. Unlike conventional processes of diagnosis that management consultants usually follow which involve looking for data and numbers to obtain insights, the U-process involves a lot of listening to people to supplement the gathering of data.

The second movement, at the bottom of the U, was called 'presencing': tapping into—becoming fully present to—a deeper knowing about one's role in the system. This is a critical step in the process, influenced by Jaworski's and Senge's personal experiences with meditation processes in eastern spiritual traditions. This is akin to personal mastery in the five disciplines, but much deeper. In fact, all participants in the U-process must spend a day and a night, or even more, in complete isolation in nature—on a hilltop or on the seashore to clear their minds.

The third movement, ascending on the right side of the U, was called 'realizing': acting from a place of deeper knowing to bring forth a new reality.

The consulting project in India was sponsored by a large multinational company with a long presence in India along with three of India's largest domestic companies. A US philanthropic organization that wanted to support Adam's consulting company to develop a new consulting methodology to solve some of the world's most challenging problems, paid the consultants' fees. The four companies, several NGOs and the government of Maharashtra assigned their people to a multi-stakeholder team that Adam led through the U-process. They named their project 'The Bhavishya Alliance' (Bhavishya means future), because the health of little children affects their development, and their development will have significant effects on India's future.

In the first stage, going down the 'sensing' side of the U, the team gathered knowledge about what was causing malnutrition to persist in India. They found many causes, not just the lack of good food. For example, poor sanitary conditions result in diarrhoea and loss of nutrients from the body. Another cause is, when families are very poor and food is limited, they prefer to feed the boys, who they hope will grow strong and earn for the family. Therefore, girls are malnourished and remain weaker, which in turn affects the health of the children they produce when they come of age.

All members of the team went into the mandatory isolation at the bottom of the U. Adam invited me to meet them afterwards. They had been moved by the poverty they had seen during their 'sensing' journey, and their introspection into the purpose of their lives while 'presencing', had made them very committed to implement a solution for chronic malnutrition.

I met the team again some months later, when they were struggling to climb up the 'realizing' side of the U. The solutions they had developed required their organizations—their NGOs and their companies—to understand the roles they must play to solve the systemic problem of malnutrition. The team members from the NGO side did not find the engagement of the rest of their own organization with Bhavishya's objectives as difficult as did the team members from the corporate world. In fact, some of the corporate team members became so unhappy with their company's lack of empathy for the cause of the underprivileged people that they later left their companies to create small NGOs of their own.

The business of the NGOs was to serve the people for whom Bhavishya was set up. Their purpose was aligned with Bhavishya's purpose. The business of business corporations, however, is business. Business organizations are constructed to serve one purpose, which is to extract profit for their owners from the use of resources—environmental resources as well as human resources. Although, many of them conduct some CSR work alongside their core business and spend a small part of their revenues on it. The Indian CSR law requires corporations to spend just 2 per cent of their profits on CSR, which is less than 0.2 per cent of their revenues assigned to those working on CSR, while the rest of the organizations, including the top brass, are focused on the 98.8 per cent.

It was no wonder that the corporate members with Bhavishya found that others in their organizations, including the top brass, did not share the passion that had been ignited in them by the 'presencing' they had experienced at the bottom of the U. I had observed a similar angst a few years before, amongst some executives who had attended IA's personal mastery programmes. They had realized that the purpose they wanted to dedicate their lives to was not aligned with the purpose of the organization they served.

The poet Robert Frost explains how organizational boundaries can constrain us. He begins his poem *Triple Bronze* with:

The Infinite's being so wide
Is the reason the Powers provide
For inner defense my hide.

Our body, and our skin that covers it, are provided by nature as a container for a spirit within. Contemplative and meditative traditions in all religions, eastern as well as western, provide ways to release the spirit from the cage of the body. Similarly, at the bottom of the U process, potential change-makers must expose themselves to the Infinite, with only their 'hides' to protect them and ignite their own spirit within.

Frost then points to boundaries that humans create and get trapped within:

For next defense outside
I make myself this time
Of wood or granite or lime
A wall too hard for crime
Either to breach or climb.

Then a number of us agree on a national boundary—

And that defense makes three
Between too much and me.

A nation is an abstract idea. When nations try to delineate their physical boundaries with beliefs about who should be included in the nation and who should not, who should be permitted to stay and who should be allowed to come and settle temporarily within the boundaries, disputes arise within a physically demarcated country. Israel is a land that has been recently demarcated as a homeland for Jews. The need for this new land arose because some Germans had decided that Jews, who had lived with them for generations, did not belong to their nation.

Human beings live within their hides and their homes and within the boundaries of countries. However, they spend most of their lives working within organizations. Organizations have rules about who is an insider and who is not. ('Hire and fire', to admit and eject, is a crude way of determining membership of an organization.)

Organizations want to create an identity for themselves—a 'brand'. Those who work in them, no matter for how long or short a time, must be part of the brand and behave accordingly while they are in the organization. I have often found people sitting beside me in an aeroplane wearing a shirt with their company's logo emblazoned on it, or they will have a bag with the logo. Companies expect their 'members' or 'partners' (it seems it's not fashionable to refer to them as 'employees' any more) to subscribe to the company's values and to direct their lives to the company's vision.

The vision and values of a company may conflict with the vision employees have for their own lives and the values they want to live by. The tension is increased when they realize that what matters most to them, which they learnt in the 'presencing' step in the U-process, clashes with their vocation. This is the dilemma that some team members of Bhavishya had faced.

I meet many young people graduating from the best business schools whom large business corporations and management consulting companies want to hire, who are less keen to join the corporate world than young people were about twenty years ago. They want the freedom to shape their lives and to create an impact in the world, which they will not be able to do if they became absorbed in corporate brands.

Organizations—governments, corporations and international governance organizations such as the United Nations (UN) and the World Trade Organization (WTO)—are social constructions designed by humans for achieving collective purposes. Humanity is confronting huge environmental and societal challenges in the twenty-first century. UN's Envision 2030 Agenda outlined seventeen sustainable development goals (SDGs) to combat these issues. The seventeenth goal—stronger partnerships—is the key to achieving the goals. New forms of teams and partnerships are required, in new forms of organizations, networks and movements.

Change-makers with a passion to improve the world must perforce engage with the world as it is. They must understand how the prevalent system operates and in what ways the present designs of institutions are contributing to the conditions they want to change. We must all fly in the aeroplane in which we are aloft for the time being. Ergo, we have no option but to redesign the aeroplane while we are flying in it. Similarly, we must restructure the institutions which govern our lives while we work with them. I have reflected on why this is difficult to do in my book *Redesigning the Aeroplane While Flying: Reforming Institutions* (2014).

Mahatma Gandhi has been one of the greatest change-makers and an inspiration for me in my efforts to become a better consultant. He was a lifelong learner at multiple levels.

He reflected on his inner self and his values throughout his life. Many spiritual masters have done this in many civilizations through history. However, unlike these spiritual masters, he did not retreat from action to purify himself and keep himself pure. He engaged with the world because he wanted to make it good for others too—not by preaching to them but by changing the conditions which were making the world unjust and unsustainable. He promoted new designs of democratic institutions for local self-governance and new forms of business institutions owned by proprietors and entrepreneurs. His autobiography, *The Story of My Experiments with Truth* is a remarkable story of a leader in action who is continuously learning throughout his life.

Mahatma Gandhi's greatest legacy perhaps lies at the highest level. He developed a method for evolving a new design of the aeroplane in which everyone is flying together, without a violent revolution to make the change and risking the chaos that follows. His method for changing the world—a method of non-violent movements—was adopted by many others across the world and applied to the causes they cared about in their own countries.

WHAT DO CONSULTANTS REALLY DO?

Good consultants are coaches and catalysts who enable others to produce the results they want. They don't 'do it' for them.

Robert Frost's poems about the woods and farms in New England, where I lived for ten years when I had joined the world of management consultants in 1989, have inspired me. The window of my office on a hill looked over the woods around the Waltham reservoir. In the fall, the maples and oaks would put on their leafy cloaks of red, yellow, orange and scarlet brown. Gradually, they would shed the leaves revealing the water through their bare branches.

'The woods are lovely dark and deep, but I have miles to go before I sleep . . .' Frost wrote.

Frost's poems speak about nature and about the human spirit too.

One of my favourite poems is *Two Tramps in Mud Time*. The poet says he was chopping wood in his yard, preparing for a long, cold New England winter when he noticed two tramps looking over his fence. They needed work and money.

Frost says he felt guilty depriving them of work they needed to earn money; the work which he was doing for enjoyment. However, he did not give up chopping the wood.

He concludes the poem with a verse that I know by heart.

> But yield who will to their separation,
> My object in living is to unite
> My avocation and my vocation
> As my two eyes make one in sight.
> Only where love and need are one,
> And the work is play for mortal stakes,
> Is the deed ever really done
> For Heaven and the future's sakes.

Ever since I gave up being a consultant formally a few years ago, many young people have consulted me about their fledgling consulting enterprises. My young friends want to improve the condition of the poor and the less privileged people of India. They have a cause they care deeply about.

For some it is the quality of education in government schools; for others it is the dignity and well-being of sanitation workers, most of whom are from the 'backward' classes historically excluded from opportunities and rights; for others it is the care for the natural environment and the dwindling water sources, forests and grasslands on which many poor Indians depend for their livelihoods. There are some who care about the despondency of young people in the Punjab where they live, who cannot find productive work and want to immigrate to other countries or take to drugs if they cannot. There are others who care about the restoration of the dignity and the rights of Dalit women in Indian villages who, as they explain poignantly, are the least respected human beings in the country.

AV, my friend who has set up a small consulting organization in the field of education, wants to help the government make its schools better. My friend, PN, who has taken up the cause of sanitation workers, wants to make a coalition of business organizations (who have come together for the same cause of improving the lot of sanitation workers), more effective in producing the outcomes they want. MM and KS, my friends who are concerned about the environment and livelihoods of people, are helping village communities improve the management of their commons. My young friend, AC, is coaching other young people in the Punjab to build local movements of change. And AS's mission is to help rape victims in villages to get justice and then to lead local movements of change in their villages, thus making a big shift in their lives—from helpless victims to social-change leaders. AS has already built the movement in many districts of the country and wants to help others to expand it further.

All my friends are consulting in different ways for different people—for village communities, youth leaders, coalitions of business, or the government. They ask me for advice on how their work could have more impact. In other words, how they could be better consultants.

AV with his avocation for education is working alongside a large management consulting company that has a multi-year contract with a state government to improve the quality of education in schools. The consulting company wanted the government to increase its fees, with rising inflation, to compensate for the higher salaries it had to pay its own consultants. The government, hard-pressed itself, was not willing. So, the consulting company contracted with AV to provide it with three young consultants at less cost. AV thought this would be a good opportunity for his young team to learn the skills of consulting. However, he is disappointed.

He says his young consultants are working alongside the (more highly paid) young consultants of the larger company writing manuals of procedures for schools. Evidently this is what the government has hired them for, whereas the real need for improvement of schools, AV says, is to build the capacity of principals of schools and teachers and make school systems work. He worries that his consultants will not learn how complex systems are improved and the role consultants can play in them by working alongside the company's consultants. AV wants to consult to fulfil his avocation; whereas for the company's consultants consulting is only a highly paid vocation.

PN cares deeply for the cause of frontline sanitation workers. She tells me a heart-warming story of a young Dalit girl whose father cleans sewers in Mumbai. When the Covid pandemic struck and the prime minister called upon all Indians to honour the doctors and medical workers fighting on the pandemic's front lines, this girl circulated a picture of her father. She said she was very proud of him because he too was fighting the war on the front, unprotected, to make the city clean and safe for everyone. PN has induced some large companies to pool their resources to help sanitation workers. Now she must get the companies' executives to open their minds, listen to these workers and understand their realities before jumping to conclusions about how their money should be spent. They are pressing her to do the usual—that is, set up efficient systems for disbursement of their aid and count how many people have benefited. She knows this is not the right method but feels powerless to tell her clients; after all, it is their money.

AS's model of change has proven to be remarkably successful in empowering rape victims to become leaders of change. Some philanthropists want him to scale it up. They are willing to give him money to hire more people, to brand his organization and enlarge it. He is tempted to do so because he wants to help many more people. However, he fears that if he takes their money and advice, he will have to spend his time in building a large organization rather than engaging directly with the cause he cares about.

Sadly, as consulting businesses grow, consultants often lose the plot. Whereas their calling should be the growth of confidence and capabilities (and indeed independence) of their clients, they begin to measure their success by the dependence of their clients on them and by the growth of the consulting business.

Medical practitioners have the same problem. They are expected to make their patients healthy quickly. If they have done their job well, their patients should not have to see them again. This may not earn them more fees, which repeated visits and many procedures would, and they may not become richer, but they will stay true to their avocation.

When young people set out to look for careers, they are well advised to look inside themselves to listen to what their avocation is (as my young friends have). They should not be swayed towards high-paying vocations which may fill their wallets but not satisfy their souls.

Frost suggests that really good work is done—for Heaven and the future's sakes—when an avocation and a vocation become one—as two eyes become one in sight.

Consulting, when it is practised as an avocation, to be a coach or a catalyst for systemic change can be deeply satisfying. When consultants begin to measure their worth by how much their clients pay them, they would be well advised to receive the eternal wisdom of the Bhagavad Gita—'You only have a right to the work, and not to the fruits thereof.'

WHAT FACTS CAN'T TELL YOU

We must listen to 'people not like us' and understand why they believe what they do.

The CEO of a large IT company I once consulted with had a rule—'It is the rule in our company that anyone who comes to a meeting must come with facts. We don't want to hear opinions. Only God is entitled to give His opinion. The rest of us must only talk with facts,' he declared.

Peter Drucker was the most influential management consultant of the twentieth century. He consulted with CEOs of some of the largest companies in the world, and with Presidents of countries too. The Drucker School of Management in Claremont Graduate University in California is named after him. He wrote several books that became textbooks for CEOs, consultants and management students—*Managing for Results; The Effective Executive: The Definitive Guide to Getting the Right Things Done; Management: Tasks, Responsibilities, Practices;* and many more.

I read Drucker's books when I began working as a manager with the Tata Administrative Services in 1965. There were no management schools in India then. I learnt management on the job, by 'rubbing my nose on the shop floor' as I have explained in my book, *The Learning Factory: How the Leaders of Tata Became Nation-Builders,* and by reading the best books on management I could get hold of.

Drucker said that whenever he met a successful executive, he always asked for their opinion. He never asked for the facts because any smart executive will find facts that support their opinion. Drucker understood human nature and how the human mind works. The erstwhile President of the US, Donald Trump, says he is a very smart man. He tweeted his opinions throughout the day. A whole industry of 'fact checkers' was required to verify his statements. Those who like Mr Trump and those who don't like him cannot settle disagreements amongst themselves about what he says. The fact checkers are also biased. Those on his side try to show that he was right and those who oppose him are convinced he is not, even before they start fact-checking.

Social media companies know, as a fact, that it is hard to change people's opinions. Therefore, algorithms of social media platforms automatically channel the information people will like to them. In this way, they reinforce people's opinions, which is convenient, no doubt, for users of their platforms. It is very useful for advertisers too, who pay social media platforms to plant their advertisements into the minds of people most likely to want their products. That is how the social media companies make money.

The problem with directing information to people who will like it and directing different information to people who have different opinions is that it is dividing the world into 'people like us' and 'people *not* like us'. The software of social media algorithms is hardening the walls within people's minds.

Social media companies, who were hailed as ubiquitous connectors of people everywhere when they burst on to the scene at the beginning of the new millennium, are now vilified as the great dividers. Since they don't want to be regulated by governments, they are desperately searching for ways to regulate what people say on their platforms.

This is not easy. A solution is to set up some sort of committee to establish guidelines for the algorithms to follow. Many points of view must be considered to determine whether a post is objectionable. Therefore, diverse persons must be brought together. The problem will be with the composition of the committee. Diverse people representing many cultures must be in this committee for it to be credible. Conservative views, liberal views, European views, Asian views, feminine views etc.—all must be represented. How will they understand each other's perspectives and come to an agreement about what is acceptable and what is not?

The solution is that people must learn to listen to each other. If I find it hard to accept what another person says, I must ask why she believes what she is saying. I should invite her to explain her opinion—as Drucker would. Then, I should go deeper to inquire *why* she has this belief. Listening must not stop at the facts. It must go deeper from only listening to the facts to understanding the other person's reasoning. It must go even deeper to listen to *who* the other person is.

Big data analytics is becoming big business. In Industry 4.0, for which everyone must be prepared business consultants say, computers will talk to computers without consulting human beings.

Human beings must find common ground. We must learn to listen to 'people not like us'. Standing upon common human ground together, we will be able to construct rules by which we will govern our conversations and guide the algorithms of computers.

COOKIES AND LEARNING

The pace of development of technology has run too far ahead of the development of human wisdom.

I learnt how to learn as a member of a team that built a 'learning factory' in India. Sumant Moolgaokar, the chairman of TELCO, had the vision to set up a factory to produce trucks and buses which would be designed by Indians. The company had a factory in Jamshedpur in eastern India, which German engineers from Daimler Benz had designed and helped Tata to build. Under a technology transfer agreement, they had also trained hundreds of Tata managers and workers to manufacture trucks and buses to Daimler's exacting standards. The Germans had taught well, and the Indians had learnt well. Within fifteen years, the vehicles produced in Jamshedpur had over 95 per cent India-made content. The Germans were so satisfied with the quality that they exported the vehicles made in Jamshedpur as Mercedes vehicles, with the Mercedes star on their grilles, to their dealers in Sri Lanka and South East Asia, saving the freight costs for the long voyage if the vehicles were to come from their factories in Germany.

When Moolgaokar planned the new factory in Pune in western India, the country's foreign exchange reserves were very low. The government limited the import of machines and dies that were required to produce the trucks. Therefore, Tata engineers, who had learnt how to produce trucks from the Germans in Jamshedpur, would have to learn how to produce machines and dies too. This required precision engineering. Daimler Benz did not make the machines and dies it used in its factories in Germany but bought them from other companies who specialized in their production. Therefore, Tata had to find other technical partners, in Germany, the UK and Japan, who were willing to teach Tata engineers to make these products in India for a fee.

The team of young engineers and workers in Pune had to learn many new things simultaneously. Only a few had worked with the Germans in Jamshedpur. The rest had to learn how to produce components of the vehicles. And, the managers who were trained in Jamshedpur had to learn how to produce machines and tools. Moreover, since the technical agreement with Daimler Benz for fifteen years had run its course, Tata engineers would also have to learn to design new models of trucks on their own.

The Tata factories in Pune must be a 'learning factory', Moolgaokar declared. He put me in charge of manpower planning and implementation to set up processes for people to rapidly learn what they must for the company to realize its vision of creating a factory designed by Indians and run by

Indians that could compete with the world's best producers of vehicles. I have written about what I learnt about organizational learning, on the job, under Moolgaokar's visionary leadership, in *The Learning Factory: How the Leaders of Tata Became Nation-Builders.*

When I left Tata and jumped into the world of consulting in the USA in 1989, my interest in organizational learning continued. The computer industry was transforming at that time. 'Big Blue' IBM's dominance over the computer industry had ended. IBM's big machines were very expensive. Other computer manufacturers—Digital Equipment Corporation, Hewlett-Packard, Compaq, Dell and more—were developing smaller, less expensive computers. Development of computing power also shifted from hardware to software. Microsoft, Oracle and others built large businesses in software for computation, which soon became larger and more profitable than IBM.

The transformations in the computer industry enabled companies to deploy computers more widely in businesses. As businesses needed consultants to help them, so the business of consulting in information technology (IT) also took off. Computer Sciences Corporation (CSC) and Arthur Andersen expanded rapidly (the latter spinning off its computer consulting division as Accenture).

A benefit to business's bottom lines of using computers was the reduction in costs for processing information and also the speeding up of information processing by replacing clerks and accountants with computers. Michael Hammer, a professor of computer science at MIT, wrote a seminal article in the *Harvard Business Review* on re-engineering business processes which introduced BPR (business process re-engineering) into the business lexicon. 'Re-engineer your company or die' became a powerful marketing slogan for consultants in the business.

Hammer followed up his article with a book, *Re-engineering the Corporation: A Manifesto for Business Revolution,* with his co-author James Champy, in 1993, which became a bestseller. Champy, also a computer scientist, had founded a small firm, Index, which was a pioneer in consulting to businesses in the application of computers to improve business performance. Index was bought by the giant CSC, and Champy then led and built CSC Index, the management consulting arm of CSC.

Electronic computers enable 'data' to be stored and processed efficiently. They assist managers to extract 'information' which they can use to take better decisions. Therefore, consultants who advise business managers on computer applications must understand business management. This was an opportunity for management consulting companies to grow their businesses too. Whereas CSC came into IT from the field of computer science, management consulting firms, like McKinsey, BCG and ADL (where I was working), came from the domain of management science. Management consulting companies set up their own IT practices. Their pitch to clients was that clients must hire management consultants who can tell them where and for what purposes they should use computers, before they hire pure IT consultants, who would be inclined to sell them more computer power and services which may add costs without benefits for their businesses.

'Data' management helps 'information' management, and 'information' can lead to 'knowledge'. Following this, IT managers in some companies were designated as 'knowledge managers', and 'knowledge management' became a new service for many consulting companies.

The connection between 'knowledge' and 'learning' is obvious because one purpose of learning is to acquire knowledge. (Another is to acquire wisdom—which we will come to later). While the interest in knowledge management was growing, some businesses had become interested in the new field of 'organizational learning' as a way to improve their performance. Peter Senge's book *The Fifth Discipline: The Art and Practice of the Learning Organization* often found place alongside Hammer and Champy's *Re-engineering the Corporation* on CEOs' bookshelves.

My interest in learning organizations had drawn me to Senge's work and to Innovation Associates (IA). ADL and IA were also drawn together by NASA, which found resonance between ADL's technology (i.e. knowledge) management capabilities and IA's learning practices. ADL was founded as a consulting company, with its roots in MIT, to help businesses apply science and technology to create innovative products. Before consulting companies began to sell IT services, ADL's consultants were already helping computer hardware companies to design their products. Thus, ADL was connected with the emerging science of knowledge management in many ways.

Knowledge management was an emerging discipline which was of great interest to many companies in many industries in the 1990s. A national business association organized a meeting of knowledge management officers from its member companies in Babson College in Wellesley, Massachusetts, to learn from each other. Babson College's dean was formerly the dean of ADL's School of Management Development in Cambridge, Massachusetts. We had worked together before. He invited me to facilitate the meeting.

The participants had various designations on their visiting cards—knowledge managers, learning officers, and several called themselves IT managers. However, all of them were responsible for 'knowledge management' in some form or other in their companies. They made an interesting observation after they had introduced themselves. All those designated as learning officers were from the HR (human resource) side of the business, whereas those designated as knowledge managers were from the IT side.

During the workshop their differing concepts of 'knowledge management' were also revealed. The knowledge managers viewed their function primarily as managers of large and easily accessible libraries of information. Whereas the learning officers associated knowledge management with employee development.

Later, a friend in MIT gave me a paper by Brandon Gill with helpful insights into the connection between knowledge management and organizational learning. The paper brought out a story to explain how an IT-based knowledge management system had killed a thriving business.

In 1977, at the age of twenty, Debbie Fields began selling her home-baked cookies at a store in Palo Alto, California. By 1981, her company had fourteen stores. Information systems were a critical component in the growth of her business. Her husband, Randy, was a computer enthusiast whose concept was to provide expertise directly to every store from the headquarters to ensure each one of them was run exactly the same way as Debbie had run the first. As much as possible, the whole process of baking was automated, so all that the employees had to do was interact with the customers. By 1987, more than 300 stores generated earnings of $17.7 million on sales of $113 million.

Then the market changed. Ms Fields' success inspired from other cookie makers, despite a growing interest in nutrition and personal fitness with which they all had to contend. Innovations in products became necessary: the old 'cookie cutter' approach would not do.

Randy added a 'learning management' component to the weekly information reports. The stores' employees were told to ask customers for feedback about Ms Fields' cookies as well as their experience with Fields' competitors. Since there were 300 stores and a lot of feedback was expected, Randy made categories of feedback for employees to give information on—feedback on taste, size, appearance of the product, price etc.

Randy found that employees did not categorize the feedback consistently. For example, they might put comments about the size of the product in the box meant for appearance. This made his task of analysing the information more difficult. He pulled up employees who were misclassifying the information.

In spite of Randy's efforts to apply knowledge management to improve the company's products, the company's sales collapsed. In 1988, the company experienced a loss of $18.5 million—and it never recovered. By 1993, lenders took 79 per cent of the company in exchange for writing off $94 million in debt, and Debbie Fields had to step down as CEO.

What went wrong? Brandon Gill of Florida State University, whose paper my friend had given to me, studied the rise and fall of the company. He interviewed Debbie and Randy and also the employees in the stores.

The employees said the knowledge management system was the problem. They interpreted the customers' feedback in the ways they thought the customers meant it. For example, if a customer said the cookies had too much butter, which was not healthy, and no column had been provided for reporting about health-related complaints, they would put the comment in the 'taste' box. If Randy noticed the comment and he thought it was in the wrong box, the employees would be pulled up and he would set the comment aside. At the same time, employees who did not find a particular category for the feedback in the system Randy had designed, would not put it into the form at all. Thus, valuable feedback, which could have helped Debbie to improve her cookies, was lost.

The story of the discovery of a hole in the ozone layer also illuminates problems with information management systems.

The first evidence that led scientists to hypothesize that there was a hole in the ozone layer came from observations from the ground. NASA's Nimbus satellites, which had very sensitive sensors and had been circulating around the world for five years, were far better equipped than ground-based instruments to detect conditions in the atmosphere. The scientists were surprised that the satellites had not found the evidence first.

They looked at the raw data that had been stored on computer tapes for the previous five years. The evidence was there. It turned out that the computer had been systematically discarding the small evidence as spurious because its software had been programmed according to a mental model that had not allowed for such a possibility.

Our beliefs create filters through which we evaluate the evidence before us. If I have a belief that men with long beards and sunglasses are dangerous, I will put this data before me into the box labelled 'Dangerous'. However, people living in a middle eastern country, many of whose friends have long beards and wear sunglasses, will put the same data into a box labelled 'Friendly'. In fact, they may put a white man in military uniform carrying a rifle in the 'Dangerous' box, whereas an American on the streets of Baghdad will put the same data into the 'Friendly' box.

The capacities of computers to gather, store and sort information have increased by many orders of magnitude since the early 1990s when Randy helped Debbie set up the knowledge management system for her business. Big data analytics has become essential to stay in business, consultants warn their clients and offer to help them of course.

Social media companies, with huge databases, enable people to connect with almost anyone, anywhere, any time. Information floating around on their ubiquitous platforms makes people jump to conclusions, which can be very dangerous sometimes. Social media is dividing people into categories of 'people like us' and 'people not like us'. Social media companies are being called upon by many countries' governments to weed out 'objectionable' information. 'One man's meat is another man's poison', as Thomas Middleton, the English playwright, said in 1604. Who is to decide what is objectionable and what is not?

Testifying before the US House Committee on Science, Space and Technology on Artificial Intelligence (AI), Fei-Fei Li, chief AI scientist at Google Cloud, explained that while algorithms that drive AI may appear neutral, the data and applications that shape the outcomes of those algorithms are not. She said, '(AI) deep learning systems are bias in, bias out.'* Shannon Vallor, a philosopher at Santa Clara University, whose research focuses on the philosophy and ethics of emerging sciences and technology, has been engaged by Google Cloud as a 'consulting ethicist'. She agrees with Fei-Fei Li, saying, 'There are no independent machine values. Machine values are human values.'

---

* Article by Jessi Hempel, *Wired*, 13 November 2018, https://www.wired.com/story/fei-fei-li-artificial-intelligence-humanity/

Information technology has given human beings enormous power to manage data and information. AI machines can learn by themselves by discovering patterns in the data. However, they do not have the wisdom to take ethical decisions. Ethical decisions require judgements about what is morally right or wrong; not only what is logically right or wrong. AI machines can take logical decisions; they are not equipped to take ethical decisions for which they need wisdom. The wisdom they need is what philosophers search for, which is an understanding of the place of human beings in the larger scheme of the universe, and also what responsibilities humans have towards all other human beings and all of nature's creations too.

Science and technology have given us the hubris that we can overpower nature, extract from it whatever we want and discard into it what we consider useless. The processes by which we destroy nature and extract resources from it add to the GDP of the country, and the processes by which we dump garbage back into nature also add to GDP. The production of weapons to destroy others adds to GDP and the production of weapons to defend ourselves adds to GDP too.

Technology has given humans considerable power over nature and significant power over each other. But technology has run too far ahead of man's wisdom to manage it. If humans do not acquire the wisdom to control it soon, technology can destroy the Earth, and man will be destroyed too.

STORIES TO THEORIES

Beliefs, which may even be unfounded, cause people to act in the ways they do, and their actions founded on those beliefs cause things to happen.

Complex ideas are difficult to communicate. Therefore, young consultants are trained to convey a complex idea, preferably broken into bullet points, on PowerPoint slides. Another way to convey a complex idea is to tell a story. Many points of view are interwoven into a story. Since reality is a rich combination of many perspectives, stories can represent reality more accurately than a slide with bullet points can. People get the point of a good story even when it is not bulleted for them. In fact, years later, they remember the point of the story *because they remember the story*.

Reality is complex because it is created by combinations of many different forces and also by the interactions of many people who have different perspectives. Stock market analysts on TV programmes show the market trends of stocks with colourful graphs bouncing around on the screen. They say that one must understand the 'fundamentals' that are causing those trends. The movements of stock markets are caused by 'sentiments' and 'moods', they add. The story of the stock market is a complex story combining different types of forces: some in the physical world of demand and supply of products which can be quantified, others in the realm of emotions which cannot be quantified. In reality, all the forces, qualitative and quantifiable ones, are woven into the behaviour of the stock, but the limitations of graphs cannot reveal all. Therefore, it is often better to communicate reality as it is—as a story—rather than as graphs of numbers or slides with bullet points. A story helps listeners to understand what is really happening.

I have narrated many stories in this book. There is a pattern in them. My stories are about people—clients, who have emotions and beliefs; and consultants, who are also people with emotions and beliefs, although their clients expect them to always be 'objective' and rational in the advice they give.

There is a point in these stories, which is, human beliefs and emotions are strong forces shaping the condition of organizations and societies.

A good physician understands how all the parts of the human body work together and he must address it as a whole even if the problem for which he is called is only in one part of it, such as the heart of which he is a specialist, because he must ensure that his treatment of the heart does not cause any damage to other organs of the body. Good physicians also know that the mind influences the condition of the body.

They should keep the whole system in their view when they prescribe any solution. Sadly, doctors often do not do so because they specialize in the treatment of only a small part of the body. They do not have a 'whole system view' of their patients' condition.

Doctors who work on human bodies must also understand how the minds within the bodies can have a profound effect on the physical health of a person. Similarly, consultants too must understand how the beliefs and emotions of people can have profound effects on the health of organizations and societies whose condition they are expected to improve.

Systems thinking helps consultants to see the whole picture. It helps them to see the interactions between different parts of the system, as the consultants in the training programme in Germany had learnt. Good consultants, like good general physicians, must be systems thinkers. They are generally not, as the story, 'All for One and None for All', about the consultants' training programme in Germany showed.

I will now explain another side of systems thinking which explains how human beliefs and emotions contribute to the trends of events we see in the world around us.

Lenses through which we see the world

Our beliefs are the lenses through which we make sense of what we see. They influence how we think about others. For example, if I have a belief that men with long beards wearing dark glasses are likely to be dangerous, my instant reaction on seeing such a man will be caution, even if the person may be a good friend who I had last seen years ago and who has, meanwhile, put on more weight and changed his dress habits.

My belief that men with beards and dark glasses are dangerous will become my established belief if I have been mugged by men with beards and dark glasses. My mind connects the dots and sees a pattern—men with beards wearing dark glasses are muggers—and the next time I see one, I am instantly alert, even if it happens to be my friend.

We must think fast to avoid danger. Nature provides all animals, humans included, the ability to make instant judgements whether to 'fight or flee'. It helps them to survive.

My brain is able to make judgements very fast because it is assisted by another part of the brain which thinks slowly. This part stores data about my experiences. It sees patterns and it provides me with hypotheses to guide me—such as, men with beards and dark glasses are dangerous.

My beliefs are also shaped by the beliefs of others whom I listen to and respect, for instance, my parents who have passed on to me what they had learnt about how to make good judgements. Perhaps, they had had bad encounters with men with beards and dark glasses and they thought it was their responsibility to save me from harm, so they taught me to emulate them and avoid such men. Or, they were told by people they trusted about the bad experiences they had. Thus, some beliefs become pervasive in society and are hard for any individual to cause a change by themselves.

Breaking vicious cycles

A belief that workers are lazy and that they cannot be trusted can develop in my mind from my own experience. Or, it can be transferred to it from the experience of others. If I have this belief, I will supervise workers more closely than I really need to.

Similarly, workers may harbour a belief that supervisors never trust their workers. So when I, as a supervisor, check my workers frequently, which I believe is the job of a good supervisor, the workers' beliefs are reinforced. If they use their initiative to make an adjustment, they fear they risk being chastised for not following rules. Therefore, they begin to wonder if there is any point in taking any initiatives on their own. And since they do not, it reinforces the supervisor's belief that workers are lazy. Thus, beliefs solidify in the minds of both workers and supervisors. A system of mutual mistrust is locked in place.

The beliefs of supervisors and their managers about the inherent laziness and untrustworthiness of workers guide the design of management systems. Supervisors are provided with sticks and carrots in the form of professionally designed disciplinary systems and reward systems to extract better performance from their workers. In this way, beliefs about the inherent laziness of workers become hard-wired into the designs of management systems and become even harder to change.

What if a supervisor were to suspend his own belief temporarily and try an experiment to encourage workers to make suggestions for improvement? The workers may respond favourably and the supervisor will see new evidence that might change his belief. He may experiment more often, giving more workers freedom to make improvements. On their part, the workers may begin to change their own generalizations about all supervisors on seeing a supervisor trust them. Thus, a vicious cycle of action and reaction, which had hardened into mistrust, can change direction, and slowly trust can be built again.

The insight from this story, for managers and for consultants, is that *human beings act themselves into new ways of thinking as often as they think themselves into new ways of acting*. Therefore, if you want to change the way the world is working, you must act accordingly within your own sphere of influence. Change-makers must follow the advice of Mahatma Gandhi, one of the greatest change-makers in recent human history, who advised, 'Be the change you want to see in the world.'

Levels of systems

Systems thinking requires attention to what is going on beneath the surface and at the backs of our minds while we think and act.

The 'facts' visible to us are caused by forces that may be invisible until we consciously apply our minds to them. In the example just discussed, evidence of laziness and reluctance of workers is visible to the supervisor, as well as to any 'objective' observer. What is going on inside the minds of workers—the 'subjective' part—is not. Similarly, evidence of harshness of supervisors is visible; their beliefs are not.

In between the visible behaviour and real beliefs of people are structures of organizations and systems that are designed to enable the system to perform well. The designs of these systems are founded on beliefs too. HR managers treat human beings as a 'resource' for the enterprise, like any other resource. HR management systems are usually designed with the belief that employees must be managed firmly.

The architecture of systems

It's a given that human beings are different from machines because they have emotions and passions and an ability to learn what they want to. Therefore, efficient leaders engage the people in their enterprise to create a shared vision for their enterprise. 'Shared visions' bring more energy into the transformation of an organization than 'visions shared', as explained in the story *The Vision Thing*.

Professional HR and communications managers may assist a CEO to develop and communicate a vision. However, real change happens, as we have seen in that story, when people are *committed* to the vision rather than *compliant* with the CEO's well-articulated vision. A vision shared by a CEO which appeals to employees can evoke *compliance,* which is good, but not as good as *commitment*. A person committed to a cause voluntarily, looks for people to form partnerships with and will cooperate with others to convert the shared vision to reality.

Professional HR managers are hired to instal constructive HR management systems. As a first step, the organization must give every employee a role description or job specification so that the employee knows what is expected of them. A job specification enables *formal compliance*. It is not a bad thing because it is logical to have requirements clearly specified. However, the nature of compliance begins to shift qualitatively from commitment to a vision to compliance with the rules and requirements of an organizational machine.

HR professionals devote a lot of time to designing performance management systems. The performance of employees in their roles must be judged objectively. Incentive systems are designed to reward high performers. Also, there must be penalties for non-performers, professionally administered of course. Employees caught within professionally managed HR systems respond to incentives, as they are expected to. Therefore, they may give *grudging compliance* to the CEO's vision if shared with them.

When the spirit of commitment is absent and when the rules and incentives don't work well, employees don't comply with the rules willingly. Therefore, supervisors must supervise them more closely, and HR managers must help supervisors resolve disputes—professionally of course.

An HR system which is not designed to energize commitment can 'professionally' create an organization run with principles of compliance. It may also produce more evidence of lazy workers who need to be managed professionally, justifying the need for more professional (and highly paid too) HR managers!

Systems designed by professionals lock into place their beliefs about human nature and about how the world works. Transformational change begins with an examination of the underlying beliefs with which policies and institutions are designed.

A fundamental belief, and an erroneous one, on which mainstream economic models have been built is that human beings are purely self-interested and rational. Whereas, we can see the evidence all around us—and within ourselves too—that we have emotions and that we can care deeply for others too.

CREATING A BETTER WORLD

CHANGING THE WORLD

THE VISION THING

It is not what *a vision is, but how it is shaped that gives it the power to transform an organization.*

Harley-Davidson motorcycles are symbols of US masculinity and Harley Owners Groups (HOG) roar along the US highways in the summer. However, Harley-Davidson, the proud US company founded in 1903 in the heartlands of the US in Milwaukee, Wisconsin, was brought to its knees in the 1980s by the invasion of Japanese motorcycles. The Japanese bikes were quieter, sleeker, more fuel efficient and less expensive. The Harley-Davidson company came close to extinction, unable to compete.

Harley-Davidson came roaring back, however. The story of the turnaround of the company by its CEO, Richard F. Teerlink, became a business legend. Teerlink wrote an article about it, Harley's Leadership U-Turn, in the *Harvard Business Review* (July-August 2000). He also wrote a book, *More than a Motorcycle: The Leadership Journey at Harley-Davidson.*

Teerlink says: 'We needed to create an environment at Harley where *everyone* took responsibility for the company's present and its future. I knew that such an approach wouldn't come naturally to Harley. After all, our crisis had been managed with an unmistakable top-down approach, as is so often the case with turnarounds. But now that times had changed, so, too, could our way of doing things. I believed then, and still do, that people are an organization's only sustainable competitive advantage.'

My manufacturing consulting team in ADL was working with Teerlink in the mid-1990s to improve the company's supply chain to reduce its costs of manufacturing and inventory, increase uptime of its assembly lines and ensure availability of spare parts in its service centres. This required good data management for systems improvement. One day, while at the job, I got an insight into Teerlink's approach to people management.

I was with him in his office in Milwaukee with my colleagues when his secretary said a reporter from the *Wall Street Journal* wanted to see him urgently. The reporter's plane from New York had been delayed and he had to return in the afternoon. Could Mr Teerlink see him immediately, she asked?

We got up to leave but Teerlink asked us to stay. 'It will only take a few minutes,' he said. 'He has come to ask me about the "vision thing".'

While Teerlink was putting Harley-Davidson back into competition, another turnaround story was unfolding in IBM. 'Big Blue', the iconic computer company, was in trouble, though not from the Japanese. It seemed to have lost the plot in the computer industry. While IBM made the most powerful computers in the world, smaller American companies were changing the shape of the computing industry. Digital Equipment Corporation on the East Coast and Hewlett-Packard on the West Coast were producing very efficient smaller computers, and Microsoft was on the way to build the world's largest software company.

IBM's board appointed Louis V. Gerstner, who had turned around American Express, as its CEO. When Gerstner unveiled his vision for IBM, it felt flat. A technology journal reported: 'The long-awaited "vision statement" by the IBM chairman, Lou Gerstner—a very long speech, full of typical "IBM speak"—turned out to be much ado about nothing. The mountain shook, [but only] a mouse was born."* Gerstner recovered from the media's criticism by declaring that the 'last thing the company needs right now is a vision'. He said the company needed a strategy. Gerstner went on to transform IBM, a remarkable turnaround story that he recounts in his book, *Who Says Elephants Can't Dance*.

The *Wall Street Journal*'s reporter had come to find out why Teerlink's vision was more compelling than Gerstner's. He asked Teerlink for a copy of the company's vision statement. Teerlink opened his drawers and pretended to look for it. He apologized and told the reporter, 'Everyone has it. You want to meet some employees while you are here, my secretary tells me. Why don't you ask anyone you

---

* Bob Djurdjevi, *Annex Bulletin*, 25 March 1994.

interview. I am sure someone can give it to you.' The reporter left to go around the factory and Teerlink proceeded with the interrupted meeting about the supply chain.

Ninety minutes later, as we were wrapping up our meeting, the reporter reappeared. Teerlink asked him if he had found the vision statement. 'The surprising thing is,' the reporter said, 'no one had the vision statement. But everyone had the vision!'

He said he had met several workers in the factory and others in the office and all of them told him what the vision was, in their own words. They also explained to him how they were applying the vision in their work.

Vision statements had become a popular management tool in the 1990s. Consultants were hired to craft an appropriate vision statement with the right words in it. Communications experts designed campaigns to roll out the vision internally and externally. The vision statement was laminated and displayed around the company. Videos were circulated for employees to hear the vision in the CEO's own voice. In these ways a well-crafted vision was shared with the employees.

A 'vision shared' is not the same as a 'shared vision', Teerlink pointed out. A vision shared is top-down. It may not excite employees far away from the CEO's office, who would not have his perspective. Whereas a vision for inspiring employees to do their best must connect with their aspirations in their own lives.

Often CEOs express their overarching vision for the company in terms of how it will be valued by investors—a billion-dollar or ten-billion-dollar company in ten years—or some such goal. It is hard to imagine a blue-collar worker waking up in the morning and saying, 'I am really looking forward to my day because I want to make my company a billion-dollar company in the stock market!' Stock market valuations may matter a lot to owners of the company, perhaps it is the only thing that matters to many investors. However, the stock price cannot motivate a worker who gets nothing out of it. Workers simply want to be proud to be a part of a great company and to work in a great team, like players of sports teams who give their best to win a match against a tough opponent and come home to proudly tell their children and grandchildren why the day they played well, even if they lost narrowly, was one of the best in their lives.

One slide I have most often used as a consultant is a picture of two broad cylinders side by side. Within one cylinder are many arrows pointing in different directions. 'This is what it probably feels like in your organization,' I suggest to people within a company or a government department. 'The arrows are all very good people,' I explain, 'as you are, but often, it appears as if you are not aligned and are working at cross-purposes too. I wonder whether you have ever experienced a situation like this.' Always, everyone nods.

Above the other cylinder is a magnet. All the arrows within it are turned upwards towards the magnet. 'Have you, at any time in your life, felt something like this, maybe, when you were playing in a sports team or in a theatre production or on a project at work?' I ask. They nod again and agree that it feels much better when one is working with others towards a common goal.

The magnet is a shared vision of the goal to be achieved by everyone working together. I pose another question. 'What if I lift the magnet much higher above the people in the cylinder? Will they still be drawn towards the goal?'

'No, they will not,' the audience responds. 'The magnetic force must touch something within them for it to change their orientations,' they explain.

That is why visions made from the perspective of the CEO, in his office twenty floors above the people working on the ground floor, will not inspire them, I explain.

For a vision to move people to give their best, it must contain expressions of what they care deeply about. They must find their aspirations expressed in it for it to inspire them. Therefore the creation of a shared vision must begin with listening to what people within the organization cherish and are concerned about.

The creation of a shared vision does not require communications experts. It requires a CEO who listens well to his people and can touch their hearts, which Teerlink seemed to have done very well, as the reporter found.

THE HARLEY TEST

Employees should shape their vision and feel it, not be told what the company's vision is.

Bharat Petroleum Company Ltd (BPCL), an Indian petroleum company in the public sector (i.e. a company listed on the stock market, but government-run), engaged IA and ADL in the mid-1990s. BPCL asked its consultants for help to improve its ability to compete with international petroleum companies which the government intended to allow into the Indian market with the progressive opening of the Indian economy following the major economic reforms of 1991.

   U. Sundararajan, the visionary chairman of BPCL, wanted his company to become a 'fast learning organization' so that it could catch up with the performance standards of international companies and stay ahead of them too. His problem was that his team of direct reports was not aligned with his vision. They did not have his passion for change. The two senior-most directors, who were to retire in a couple of years, were the most cynical about his new-fangled ideas about 'learning organizations' in which all employees learn together and work together to bring about the transformation of the organization.

Sundararajan didn't have the kind of levers to motivate his directors, which the boards and CEOs in the private sector did. He could not offer them handsome performance bonuses and stock options. His salary as well as the salaries of all employees in the company were controlled by government rules. Sundararajan asked me to help him. He convened a meeting of the directors in the Taj Mahal Hotel, on a Saturday when I was in Mumbai from the US.

We were a small group of only eight, seated comfortably on sofas in a luxurious private meeting room in the Taj. After the preliminary introductions, I asked everyone how many years remained until their retirement. The youngest director had twenty; the two senior-most only two.

I asked them to shut their eyes and envision what they might be doing five years from then. Perhaps travelling in a plane from Mumbai to Delhi in business class, if they were still working. Or, perhaps sitting on a bench in the park in the morning with other retired persons. The oldest directors smiled—they could foresee that.

I presented a hypothetical situation: Suppose the person sitting next to you, in the plane or in the park, opens the morning paper and there is a headline story about BPCL. You have already introduced yourself to the person near you and they know that you are working in BPCL or had retired as a director on its board. What would you like that story to say about BPCL? I asked them. Please write in bullet points what you would like to read in the story.

They became quiet and wrote thoughtfully. I asked them to share what they had written. They were inspired by what they heard from each other.

Then I asked them to consider what must happen in the next five years for the company to achieve what they had described in their vision. I introduced the concepts of accelerated organization learning to them which IA and ADL were proposing to teach them for the all-round transformation of the company. I told them that the transformation would require all the employees, including the directors, to learn and improve their capabilities.

One of them asked how long it would take to change a company of their size, with a few thousand employees around the country. It depends, I said, on how much passion there is for change within the company and how much resistance there is to it. It was the job of the people at the top to inspire people to make changes happen.

One of the two directors, due to retire soon, said that he did not want to see himself sitting on a bench in the park five years from then and to have to admit to his neighbour that he had been with BPCL if the story about BPCL was not a good one. In fact, whatever would be done in BPCL in the next two years would have to be his legacy. He was the HR director. He wanted to know what he must do to accomplish the transformation of BPCL in the next two years.

I told them the story of the turnaround of Harley-Davidson and the power of a shared vision. I proposed that each of them should assemble their own teams in the coming week and ask them, as I had, what they aspire to make happen in the company. And, to ask *their* own direct reports to assemble *their* teams in turn and so on to cascade down until they had listened to everyone, even to the operators in their remotest supply depots.

I proposed they take the 'Harley test' in six months' time. Supposing a reporter from the *Economic Times* were to visit the company's remote depots and ask the employees there what the company's vision was, what would they say to him?

They understood what must be done, and why, to enable a rapid transformation in the company. However, they were concerned that neither they, nor their subordinates, would be able to conduct such 'vision' meetings with their colleagues the way I had. The HR director proposed that a few potential leaders in the company, who had already been identified, should be rapidly trained to facilitate such meetings. As the first step in the transformation process an IA consultant trained them, and they got the process of creating a shared vision for BPCL under way.

A few months later, the directors decided to conduct the Harley test on themselves. They fanned out across the country to see if employees down the line had the vision. They returned and reported what they had learnt. The chairman asked me to listen in.

They reported the enthusiasm for change that had infected the whole company. There was no 'vision statement' written anywhere, yet the vision of what BPCL would soon become was everywhere.

The HR director had gone to the remotest supply depot where an operator had told him that the vision had given him great hope for the future. The HR director pulled out a piece of paper on which he had noted a poem that the worker had shared explaining the power of the vision. The worker had recited the poem 'The Dawning' by Sahir Ludhianvi, a famous Indian poet.

> From the horizon
> In the awakening of dawn
> The path comes to me
> Strengthened in the dawning.
> Frozen crust on the ground
> Shimmers in growing light:
> At my feet, beneath the frost, I see
> Breaking shoots of green

The operator said that he and his colleagues were following the path they could now see towards their vision—the light on the horizon. His colleagues explained the steps they were taking in their depot. The HR director was pleased to report that transformation was already under way, bottom-up.

The acceleration in BPCL's performance was remarkable. Within three years, stock market analysts were pointing out how much BPCL's growth of revenues and profits and its stock price had exceeded that of its competitors.

Public-sector companies are generally considered to be stodgy compared with their private-sector competitors. BPCL's internal facilitators of change, who had been trained by IA, were invited to present how they had brought about the transformation, at a meeting of the International Society of Organizational Learning in California. They were the only team from a developing country to be invited and the only one from a public-sector company too.

THE HORSE BEFORE THE CART

People come first; implementation follows.

JS, a BCG consultant in India, asked me if he could ride with me in the car to the airport. We were flying from Mumbai to Delhi; I, for a meeting with CII, he, to organize the implementation of the strategy that BCG had developed for a large public-sector bank. This was sometime in 2000. BCG had set up a small consulting outfit in India. JS was one of the pioneers who had taken up the challenge of growing BCG's operations when the benefits of management consulting were not yet fully understood by Indian corporates. Moreover, McKinsey, which had come to India a decade before, had taken a large share of the fledgling market.

JS got to the point as soon as we were in the car. 'How can I make 1,00,000 employees change their minds?' he asked. JS had worked in the Indian banking industry before he joined consulting. He had taken up the challenge of building a market for BCG in the banking sector. With the support of a senior partner from Europe, he had sold a large project to one of India's largest public-sector banks to implement its turnaround strategy. It was a breakthrough for BCG in India.

In the first phase, BCG had developed the strategy for the bank, which required a change in the bank's culture. The board had accepted it. The bank's employees, right down the line, would have to adopt new technologies, become more efficient in their work and more customer-oriented. JS was in charge of a small team of young consultants to implement this strategy.

JS's question was, how can five consultants change 1,00,000 minds? I thought of an old joke—how many consultants are required to change a light bulb? My short answer to JS was, five consultants cannot change 1,00,000 people. The people must change their own minds.

JS was aware of the consulting project I had led with BPCL, an Indian public-sector company in the petroleum sector, where the culture was remarkably transformed without applying any of the usual HR management levers of financial reward for good performance and penalty for failure. Reward-and-penalty strategies cannot be applied because personnel management rules in public-sector organizations are inflexible. Lifetime employment and promotion by seniority are the norm. Yet, the company had transformed its culture and became the best performing company in the industry within three years. (This has been described in a previous story—*The Harley Test*.)

BPCL's turnaround had been remarkable, as was the consulting approach that was adopted. U. Sundararajan, the chairman, had insisted that he did not want a team of consultants to implement the change (nor even to devise the strategy); the company's employees would implement the change themselves. He expected ADL (with IA), the consulting company he had engaged, to train BPCL employees and its directors to change the 'light bulbs' themselves.

Consulting companies earn their revenues by deploying large teams, of mostly young consultants, to implement change in their client organizations. The companies' fees are based on the time the consultants spend on the job. Therefore, the companies want to deploy a large number of consultants for longer periods. In fact, a consulting company's partners are rated by the size of the projects they can sell their clients (which means, how many consultants the client can be induced to pay for).

Sundararajan understood this ploy. He said he was willing to pay for the transfer of the knowledge of how transformation is brought about in a company but not for consultants to do the work. He devised a win-win contract. He said he would pay a large lump sum fee for 'knowledge', which would be in the form of manuals in which IA's consultants would codify the processes and tools they would teach a large internal team of change-makers in his company. These change-makers would do the work, coached by a couple of senior consultants from IA. However, the lucrative fee would be linked to performance. Only if the company achieved the culture-and-performance change, they would pay the fees. The change was made, and the fee was paid.

It was one of the most lucrative consulting contracts for ADL. Its costs for implementation were small because very few of its own staff were deployed, so the profit margin was very high. At the same time, the petroleum company achieved its aim at less cost, the proof of which was that its competitors had paid much more to other consulting companies in conventional contracts—i.e. large teams and large fees—and yet had not been able to change as fast.

In Sundararajan's model, consultants need not light up every street light—as lamplighters were wont to do before the invention of electricity. A good consultant must set up a system whereby many minds will change themselves—like electric lamps that come on simultaneously along the street.

What you have to understand, I suggested to JS, is what inspires human beings to change their outlook, change their own behaviours and want to acquire new skills. I explained the difference between a vision shared top-down and a shared vision amongst employees of what they want to achieve in their lives. JS offered me his notebook. I drew the picture (which I have explained in the story, *The Vision Thing*) of the two cylinders, with the arrows in them and with a magnet above one of them drawing people towards itself.

CEOs (and their consultants) know the power of a vision. However, they have it backwards: they craft the vision first and then communicate it to employees, rather than engage employees with the crafting of the vision.

Large consulting projects usually begin with the strategy first and then its implementation. This can work when the targets of change are mostly numbers on a balance sheet or arrangements of factories and machines. Numbers and machines have no emotions, whereas human beings do. Therefore, if the transformation of the organizations' performance requires human beings to change their outlooks and behaviours, their aspirations must be fulfilled by the transformation or they will resist it.

My clients have often asked me, when is the right time to begin implementation? I tell them, on Day One. Implementation of transformation of social systems—countries as well as organizations—begins with the engagement of people. Therefore, when you have the gleam in your eye to bring about a large transformation, go out and engage the people. Not only should they have a desire for change in their minds, they will also have the best ideas about how to make the changes necessary in their parts of the organization and contribute to the overall transformation.

Ambitious transformation projects often put the 'cart before the horse'—they put the vision statement before the engagement of people; they put strategy before implementation of transformation.

Soon after my conversation with JS sometime in 2000, B. Muthuraman, then MD of Tata Steel, asked me to meet him. Tata Steel is the doyen of Indian industry. It was set up by Jamsetji Tata at the turn of the nineteenth century in spite of non-cooperation by the British who ruled India at the time. This was before Mahatma Gandhi led a nationwide Non-Cooperation movement against the British which eventually led to India's freedom. Tata had been the advocate for *atmanirbhar* (self-reliance) in Indian industry over a hundred years before Narendra Modi, the Prime Minister of India, declared a vision of *atmanirbhar* for India in 2020.

In fact, Mahatma Gandhi said that while he fought for India's political freedom, Jamsetji Tata fought for India's industrial freedom.

Tata Steel was different from other business enterprises in India. It was often described as a socialist enterprise rather than a capitalist one because of the orientation of its management towards its employees. Lifetime employment was the norm in Tata Steel—the concept of 'hire and fire' was anathema to its directors and managers. Yet, sometimes, changes in technologies and the emergence of new competitors can make it imperative for even a socialist enterprise to downsize its workforce.

Tata Steel faced such a moment of truth in the mid-1990s. It had engaged ADL as consultants to its senior management to consider directions for the company's future. The ADL team consisted of a few senior experts. There were no young consultants running around gathering data to make presentations to the management. The wise old consultants helped the top management to pick up the mirror themselves and to confront their own reality.

Dr J.J. Irani, then MD of Tata Steel, (before Muthuraman), accomplished the downsizing of the Tata Steel workforce from over 70,000 employees to only 40,000, without any employee throwing a single stone in protest. The union cooperated with the management. The union, in turn, had the support of the workers because Tata Steel went beyond the requirements of the law to take care of the needs of those workers who would have to prematurely leave the company's services. The employees were given generous pensions immediately upon their dismissal. Their families were assisted to rehabilitate themselves, with training and employment for younger members wherever feasible. Though all this would add to the company's costs for a few years, the management and the union knew that it would help the company to become leaner and fitter for competition in the long run.

Muthuraman, who had become the MD of Tata Steel upon J.J. Irani's retirement, was a long-time veteran of the company, having joined it as a young graduate engineer in 1965. He had been with the company through many moments of anguish and recovery over four decades.

There were tough times in the 1960s, when he had joined the company, because the government was investing national resources in three large steel plants in the public sector. They were equipped with the latest technologies from Germany, Britain and the Soviet Union. Tata Steel devised a strategy to produce specialized steel, which required more technical expertise that Tata Steel had. The strategy also required small-size-production equipment, thus turning Tata Steel's disadvantage into a competitive advantage. Moreover, prices and margins in such specialized steel were higher than in the mass-produced steel the new government plants were designed for. However, since such products could not be sold as commodities, better marketing skills were required. Tata Steel shifted its strategy and built its competitive advantage around better customer orientation rather than low costs. Muthuraman, as the director in charge of marketing, had been largely responsible for the implementation of that transformation.

Following the trouble-free retrenchment programme implemented by Dr Irani, Muthuraman felt the company needed a vision of what it could achieve in the coming years.

Every year, the birth anniversary of Jamsetji Tata, the founder of the Tata Group, is celebrated enthusiastically in Jamshedpur on 3 March. Workers take out processions with floats and flowers. The chairman of the Tata Group comes to Jamshedpur from the headquarters in Mumbai, garlands Jamsetji's statue and addresses the employees. This would be a suitable occasion to announce the new vision, Muthuraman thought. He had some ideas about what the vision should be and invited me to discuss these ideas with him. He wanted the vision to inspire all employees and wanted me to guide him through the process he should adopt.

Muthuraman gathered the small team he had assembled to design the vision. I conducted a small workshop and explained the five processes used for developing and communicating visions:

- The simplest is 'Telling the vision'. The CEO makes a compelling speech, or sends out a written missive, to deliver his vision to the people.

- The CEO's communications experts will advise him that this is never enough. He must 'Sell the vision' too. The vision statement must be packaged attractively and marketed effectively. The communications experts, who are generally from the world of advertising, offer their services to craft and communicate a vision. (Muthuraman had the advertising people knocking on his doors already.)

- However, as good advertisers also advise, it is wise to do a quick consumer check to test a product or marketing idea and to tweak it before a mass roll-out. Therefore, 'Testing the vision' is the next process for developing and communicating visions.
- Perhaps one should take a step back and consult some employees about what the vision should be before testing an almost completed vision idea. 'Consulting for the vision' is good. That way one can sense misalignments, if any, between the vision from the CEO suite and the perspectives of employees.
- The fifth process is 'Co-creation of the vision', whereby what matters to employees is included in the content of the vision even before it is cleverly crafted by communications experts into a product for testing before selling.

I explained the differences in the impact that visions can have on the depth and speed of transformation, depending on the process used. CEOs must choose the appropriate process to suit their own aspirations. Clearly co-creation is the most powerful one. However, it takes more time and effort than all the other methods. Since 3 March was only four months away and Muthuraman had already announced that a new vision would be unveiled on that day, he did not have enough time for co-creation. Besides, consulting with 40,000 employees, many of whom were posted in remote iron ore mines, collieries and sales offices, would not be feasible. Therefore, he should consider a combination of consulting and testing the vision.

However, Muthuraman had a gleam in his eye. The picture of the two cylinders with the magnet, which illustrated the difference in power between a vision shared and a shared vision, had inspired him. He liked the idea of the 'Harley test' of the efficacy of a vision—will employees within the organization be able to explain the vision to a visitor without an official statement of the vision plastered around in their workplaces?

'We must put the power of the horse in front of the cart to be pulled,' Muthuraman told his team. 'Let us find an innovative way to engage all employees before Founder's Day in March,' he declared.

They did. They incorporated the essential principles of consultation with co-creation into a process of company-wide participation of employees in the shaping of a vision. They took advantage of the new information and communication technology the company was installing (Tata Steel was a leader in the use of digital technologies in the Indian steel industry). In four months the vision was announced on Founder's Day; it passed the Harley test.

Tata Steel continued to make all-round improvements. It was the first integrated steel company in the world, outside of Japan, to win the Deming Grand Prize, which is considered to be the highest award in the area of Total

Quality Management. Winning the 2012 Deming Grand Prize was a testimony to the company's progress in achieving excellence in business owing to the continued engagement of all its employees.

THEORIES TO STORIES

Economic policies are being driven by theories; not founded on how human beings actually think and behave.

All systems of management and all systems of economic governance are structures which are built upon beliefs and theories.

As a picture conveys a thousand words, a picture of an iceberg in the ocean can explain the structure of complex systems. A large iceberg, which is a dense aggregation of water molecules, is difficult to move. It floats within an ocean of water molecules through which ships sail easily. But if a ship hits an iceberg, the iceberg will not shift; the ship will sink. The dense aggregation of the molecules in the iceberg gives it its power and its shape. Only one-seventh of an iceberg is visible above the water. Most of it is underwater and cannot be seen, which is why icebergs are hazardous to steer past and can tragically sink even strong ships like the Titanic in 1912.

Similarly, the events that are visible to us are most often caused by forces that are invisible to us. The combination of the forces and the events they cause compose a dense system, like an iceberg. Therefore, to understand why we see some events frequently—like recalcitrant workers and labour disputes, which we examined in *Stories to Theories*—we should look beneath the water surface to see what theories are causing those stories.

Stories to Theories analysed the beliefs that drive the design of HR management systems. We will now look at three fundamental theories on which economic policies are based.

(1) Human beings are rational and self-interested actors.

This theory presumes that human beings do not have any 'irrational' emotions and passions. Looking around us, we know this is not true. A significant part of literature, fiction as well as non-fiction, is an account of the passions and emotions of human beings when they love or fight with each other. Stripped of emotions, human beings would be easier to understand, no doubt. But they *do* have emotions and passions which need to be taken into consideration.

Some scientists believe that unless reality can be explained in mathematical equations of numbers, one cannot know the truth. Emotions and passions are not easy to measure 'objectively' because they are, well, too 'subjective'. Therefore, economists, in their efforts to be 'scientific', strip out human passions and emotions from their models. This enables them to run their complex equations on computers. Sadly, their models do not represent the world as it really is.

The American statistician Nate Silver points out in his book, *The Signal and the Noise,* that forecasts of GDP growth since 1968 by the Survey of Professional Forecasters have been right only 50 per cent of the time—no better than tossing a coin— and that economists have predicted only two out of the sixty recessions in the world since 1990 a year ahead of time. Should we keep turning to economists for guidance if they do not seem to know what is going on, was Queen Elizabeth's concern when she asked why economists could not predict the 2008 global recession. The problem is that whereas economists do not have a good model to explain the relationships between the many forces shaping societies and economies, they nevertheless want to sound like experts by adding decimal points to their predictions.

(2) A foundational model for systems of management and economic policies is Abraham Maslow's 'hierarchy of needs'.

According to Maslow, human needs form a hierarchy. At the bottom are basic *physiological* needs for food, water, etc. to keep human bodies alive. The next level is the need for *safety*—such as a house to provide shelter from the elements. Above that are needs for *love and belongingness*. Higher above is the need for *self-esteem*. Finally, on top of Maslow's hierarchy is the human need for *self-actualization*.

Economic policies are based on the flawed assumption that human beings do not seek satisfaction of their needs at higher levels until their needs at lower levels have been sufficiently fulfilled. If this were so, one would not expect to find poets writing poetry or yogis retreating to find meaning in their lives, until they were well fed and safely housed. Many poets and artists devote themselves to producing great art while remaining materially very poor, and yogis may starve themselves to achieve self-realization!

Maslow's hierarchy is quite muddled in the middle too in the realms between physiological needs and self-actualization. People seem to value love and belonging (and self-esteem too), as much as they value their material needs. Often, they will sacrifice material satisfaction for the sake of self-esteem. Human needs for esteem may be fulfilled by pride in belonging to a nation and its culture. Human history, through the ages, is replete with stories of people risking their lives for the glory of their own tribe and nation.

According to economists' interpretation of Maslow's model, lower-level needs in the hierarchy must be met sufficiently before people will seek to fulfil higher-level needs. If this interpretation were accurate, Indians would not have been motivated by their need for self-esteem to demand Independence from British rule until poverty had been removed from the country.

A fundamental question that continues to confuse economists is, how much income and consumption is sufficient to remove poverty from people's lives? The poverty level is a moving target. When basic material needs are met, people desire better standards of living. A small room with four walls and a roof over their family's heads and enough calories in the food every day may be enough to lift people out of poverty in many parts of the world. However, many people in the USA and western Europe, who have homes with two rooms, a kitchen and a bathroom and who consume enough food to put on unnecessary weight, are considered poor because they cannot afford the same levels of medical care as the rich, or possess a car, which most people in their country do.

People who do not have as many material comforts as others around them do—even if they have more than enough to satisfy their basic physiological needs—are looked down upon by their neighbours who are better off. They are made to feel poor and that breaks their self-esteem.

Capitalist economies work by inducing people to buy more commodities than they really need because consumer demand for goods drives economic growth. It attracts large investments of capital and enables investors to make more profits. Therefore, corporations create greater demand for their products by clever advertising. They brainwash consumers to buy more and consume more by associating purchase of the products with fulfilment of their need for esteem in society. The display of wealth has become the new norm: 'Wear expensive brands of clothes and sneakers and you will be the envy of other kids in school.' 'Are you still using last year's model of smartphone when others have already bought the latest one?' It doesn't matter if the existing phone serves your purpose; you must keep up with the Joneses.

By clever advertising and marketing, business corporations entice people towards irrational consumption of goods because they want them to consume more to keep the profit-wheels of businesses moving. Economists are also guilty of promoting excessive consumption because they want to increase the size of the GDP, which has become the supreme measure of the progress of countries.

(3) The 'tragedy of the commons' is another fundamental premise on which economic policies have been built.

Garrett Hardin introduced the concept of the tragedy of the commons (ToC) in economics in 1968. ToC declares that property which does not belong to individuals, cannot be and will not be cared for properly. Therefore, the best way to manage and protect any resource, according to ToC, is to privatize the ownership of all resources. Even environmental resources, such as land, forests and water, must be converted to private property to ensure their good management. ToC provides intellectual justification for the ideology of privatization of all assets, including those that the whole community should have equal access to, as well as to privatization of schools, hospitals and even prisons. It justifies the shrinking of the role of governments in managing any asset for public benefit.

Evidence from history of human beings managing their commons efficiently was set aside to propound ToC as a universal principle of economics. In 2009, Elinor Ostrom was awarded the Nobel Prize in Economic Sciences for showing that, contrary to ToC, humans are willing to, and are able to, cooperate with each other to manage forests, fisheries and lands for their common benefits.

Systems thinking teaches us that beliefs and 'theories in use', even if flawed, are the foundations on which systems of management of organizations and of economies are built. If we see trends of events above the waterline, we should look beneath it to examine the structures of the systems causing those trends. And we must look even deeper to understand the beliefs with which those structures have been built.

Policies and systems of governance founded on these wrong premises have led to systemic global problems of climate change and inequity in society which cannot be solved with these theories any longer.

THE DOUGHNUT AND THE HOLE

Social enterprises require an architecture based on the principles with which nature organizes itself.

The Covid-19 virus has battered India's economy. India's GDP reduced by 24 per cent in Q1 2021—the biggest drop amongst all countries. India has the largest number of young people in the world who are expected to provide a 'demographic dividend' to India's economic growth—provided they are educated and employed—but education and employment in the country have been shaken by the pandemic. What will their future be like? Meanwhile, millions who were employed have lost their jobs and incomes and are suffering great hardships.

Covid-19 has also revealed the abundance of spirit and energy in India's youth. They took initiatives to provide relief to the needy. Many of them had already been working in a number of social enterprises to improve health, education and livelihoods of people in the country.

India has around 4 million social enterprises registered as NGOs. There may be many more informal ones, unregistered.

Social enterprises were hit hard by the economic crisis. CSR funds have dried up because donors' businesses were hard-hit too. In an aeroplane the flight attendant instructs passengers to put on their oxygen masks first before helping others. Without sponsors, how will social enterprises, on which so many lives are dependent, find their oxygen to survive?

Many years ago, I found place mats on tables in a New York coffee shop offering good advice. The message is, 'As you go on through life, brother, keep your eyes on the doughnut and not on the hole.'

Many young people in India are on a mission to make the world better for everyone. The number of people who have set out to make a difference in the way India is developing gives me great hope. All these people with an urge to make a big impact face the same challenge—lack of monetary aid. Often it seems that the only resource they can count on is their own passion, as financial resources are becoming hard to come by. Therefore, what they need is innovations in their models of organization that can produce the outcomes they want with less financial support.

Some of these young people turn to me for advice on the strategy and design of their organizations. They expect I can guide them because I have worked for twenty years in various international consulting companies, even leading strategy and organization consulting practices in them. Also, I have served on many boards—of business corporations, NGOs, and educational institutions too. Besides, when I served as a member of India's Planning Commission, I listened to scores of leaders of civil society organizations who, while communicating their needs to me, also consulted me about their strategies.

When young change-makers set out to change the world, their aspiration often is to have 'impact on scale'. They believe that to have impact on scale they must have a large organization. They take the conventional approach, for which they can hardly be blamed because that is how it has always been done and which is what their management consultants also advise them to do.

They design an organizational structure—much like a conventional pyramid, with a board of eminent persons on top. They may even imagine a smart building in which to house their staff. They feel compelled to do this because it is the usual practice, and also because their potential funders want a plan in a conventional form. Thus, their energy gets diverted from their passion for their work (the doughnut) to building their own organization and to scurrying for funds to support it (filling the hole). When funds are hard to come by, as they generally are, they become disheartened.

The lesson is: Stay focused on the work and find innovative ways to do it which will not require much money.

'Scaling up' can kill the spirit of the enterprise

Some of the largest entrepreneurial organizations in the 'for-profit' sector began with a couple of young people in a university dorm, or in a garage, who had ideas they hoped would grow into big enterprises.

The entrepreneurs gathered a few people around them who had the knowledge and capabilities required to give substance to their ideas. When the ideas developed further, they began to increase their organizations' size and to look out for investors to support them.

Initially, the small organizations were held together by shared visions, creativity and flexibility, and minimal critical rules. As they scaled up, they became formally organized. While adopting conventional methods of organizing to scale up, they began to lose creativity and flexibility. Some of the original creators, missing the earlier spirit of entrepreneurship and creativity, left. Those who remained were bound by expectations of a large financial reward. Outside investors were attracted. They had expectations which were often not in alignment with the founders. Clashes of values ensued and governance suffered.

A tragic example of this was the flaming out of SKS Microfinance, which brought down the entire Indian microfinance industry ten years ago. It was the rising star, which tapped successfully into venture capital funds and stock markets for resources to scale up its operations. The management cultures and values of the world of profit and the world of social change are not compatible.

When financial resources are scarce in the system, innovative, 'for-profit' ventures will continue to draw investments. 'Not-for-profit' social enterprises, while tugging at potential investors' heartstrings, will not find their purse strings easy to open. Therefore, they must beware of adopting enterprise and governance models that work in the for-profit space. They must be careful when introducing 'good management' structures that will dampen the spirit of commitment and creativity.

A fundamental difference between creative enterprises 'for-profit' and creative enterprises 'not-for-profit' is the purpose of the enterprise. A business enterprise must provide products and services that people want to buy; otherwise, it will not be able to earn revenues and make a profit. The purpose of entrepreneurs who go into business is not an altruistic one only: it is to make profits. They hope the business will be highly valued by the stock market when it is listed. Before they get there, they need the support from investors, most of whom hope for an early 'exit' with big financial gains.

Social entrepreneurs need financial support too. However, their purpose in life is to help others, not to accrue financial gains for themselves.

Both business entrepreneurs and social entrepreneurs provide services to the community, and both need money. Business entrepreneurs *want* to make money: it is a marker of their success. Social entrepreneurs need money too, but only to support a public cause. Their financial size, if large, may be a warning sign that they have put on too much weight and are spending too much energy (and money) to manage their internal processes and not serving the community as much as they could.

The most important lesson for not-for-profit social-impact enterprises is this: *Do not be obsessed with the scale and brand of your own enterprise. Stay focused on its purpose.*

The scale of the outcomes that you stimulate matters; not the scale of your organization. Learn to be a catalyst. Catalysts expedite chemical processes though only a minute quantity is required to produce a dramatic change.

Learn from nature: It operates on a large scale without a large-scale organization controlling it

The Amazon rainforest is a remarkably complex system. It has lush vegetation, and thousands of species of birds, animals, insects and reptiles swarm under the canopies of tall trees. They live together, and evolve together, through rain and sunshine.

Step into the rainforest and you will be overawed by nature's creativity. Who is in charge of the forest? Who is telling all the animals, birds, insects and trees what to do and when? The answer is, nobody. And yet, every part of the forest cooperates with each other.

Nature provides clues for designing complex *self-adaptive* systems. The systems within nature operate without a boss. The parts coordinate with each other. Unlike machines and computers, natural systems are not designed by an engineer outside the system nor do they need an external controller to fix them. They evolve and grow naturally.

Some principles of organization that social enterprises can learn from nature are:

- The organization must have *permeable boundaries* so that many entities can participate in it

- It must have *requisite variety*—by including diverse points of view and diverse resources—so that it can marshal the range of capabilities it needs in order to accomplish the complex task it must carry out. (Standardization makes communication and management easy, but it kills creativity.)
- The diversity within can be a challenge. Everyone cannot be expected to agree about everything. However, there must be some essential protocols (or rules) that all must follow to enable them to work together. Such as, the few simple rules of the Internet which everyone who uses the Internet must follow to enable everyone around the world to communicate on the Internet. However, *the internal rules must be minimal and only the most essential ones retained.* If there are too many rules, the organization will require internal policing to impose the rules; then bureaucracy and compliance with rules will dampen the joy of working for a cause.

These three architectural principles for self-adaptive organizations—permeable boundaries, requisite variety and minimal critical rules—have been distilled from studies of how nature functions. Nature is a complex and yet self-adaptive system in which various sub-systems cohabit and evolve harmoniously with each other.

Human systems manifest a powerful characteristic which is not as evident in other systems and subsystems in nature. Humans want to change the world *proactively*—like social entrepreneurs with a passion to alter the world. Therefore, human beings project visions of what they want to achieve in the future, and they collectively devise strategies and technologies to realize their visions. Indeed, this is why human societies create institutions and organizations to enable them to attain their visions.

This additional feature of human systems, not noted in other natural systems, requires another design principle.

- A *shared vision* is necessary for aligning people and organizations, which, while carrying out their own business in their own ways, can collectively shape a new future for the world.

Indeed, it was the force of a shared vision of 'freedom for all' that propelled India's freedom movement, spearheaded by Mahatma Gandhi. Having won freedom, people's visions diverged and concentrated on what form of governance (more local or more 'commanding heights') the country should adopt to achieve *poorna swaraj*—economic, social and political freedom for all. A 'non-Gandhian', more centralized, path was chosen and poorna swaraj became more difficult.

In summary, four architectural principles must be adopted to create an organization with the power of a self-adaptive system to induce change in the system of governance around it. These are:

- Shared vision
- Permeable boundaries

- Requisite variety
- Minimal critical rules

(The story of the discovery of these principles is in the narrative *Out of the Box)*

All young leaders who rise with a care for a cause have the same challenge. They want to give more attention to the doughnut and not to the hole. Often it seems that the only resource they can count on is their own passion. Therefore they must apply innovative concepts of organization that are financially lean.

They must create networks and movements of change, within which they will operate as small, catalytic nodes stimulating learning amongst partners—and continuing to learn themselves—rather than attempting to create 'world-class organizations' to have impact on scale that are founded on prevalent theories of organization applied by the corporate and government sectors and even by 'large-scale' NGOs.

Models of leaders

When I returned to India from the USA in 2000, I facilitated a large 'scenario planning' exercise, which I have mentioned before in the story 'Wanted: New Solutions'. The purpose of the exercise was to determine what should be India's strategy to accelerate faster and more inclusive growth.

A large and diverse group of people, comprising economists, senior government officials, journalists, artists, businessmen, teachers, students, political leaders and others, had tackled this question. They were concerned that while India seemed to have escaped the so-called 'Hindu rate of growth' that had dogged it until the 1980s and had begun to change and grow faster since the 1990s, the improvement was not fast enough to eradicate the country's enormous problems, such as poverty, failing social services and poor infrastructure.

They used a process called 'generative scenario thinking' in which the underlying forces as well as the visible 'facts' within a complex situation are analysed. The group collectively constructed a systemic view of the Indian reality that they could not have seen from their own narrow perspectives.

India was midway through an era of coalition governments then and had a slower growth rate than China. According to many Indians, who envy the remarkable improvements in China's cities and its infrastructure, India suffers from the drag of democratic processes. Many economists opine that in poor countries economic growth should precede democracy, but in reality even India's poorest people will not give up their democratic rights. Indians, therefore, have no option but to improve the way their democracy functions by tackling two interrelated questions: What is the process by which a large and diverse democratic country can accelerate its development? And, what is the appropriate leadership model for this process?

The discussions generated four visions of processes of change and four models of leaders to consider. We are told that a picture is worth a thousand words, so images similar to India's own Panchatantra folk tales were selected to convey the essence of these models of change and leadership.

Model 1: Political leaders and experts on top (*Buffaloes wallowing*[*])

Buffaloes cooling themselves in a pond is a familiar sight in the Indian countryside—it is difficult for any buffalo to move about in the pond because they are surrounded by many wallowing buffaloes.

In a similar scenario, experts, bureaucrats and others in prominent positions are expected to determine and bring about policies and changes. But they cannot agree unanimously on what should be done; what one proposes, others oppose, and nothing much happens. India's progress is slow because it is hampered by a lack of consensus amongst various political groups and various factions of people subscribing to different ideologies.

Meanwhile, the general population waits for progress, especially young people who will need jobs when they grow up—imagine a boy watching the buffaloes from the side of the pond.

Model 2: Wealth creators and economy movers (*Peacocks strutting*)

India adopted a model of change with its economic reforms in 1991. It was an attempt to move away from the model of 'licence raj' with 'buffaloes wallowing'. The scenario the participants of the dialogue produced was called 'Peacocks

---

[*] India scenarios, published by CII/BCG in 2000.

Strutting, Birds Scrambling'. It was the story of the free market and the trickle-down effect.

In this story, a woman scatters grain in her yard for the sparrows to eat. Some pigeons arrive and push aside the sparrows, then a peacock arrives and the pigeons move aside. All the birds look in awe at the peacock and admire its finery and its size, and the sparrows hope that, after the peacock has eaten, there will be something left for them.

The peacock represents the wealthy, whose expensive clothes and lifestyles are constantly displayed in electronic and print media. They are successful because they have money. People look up to them as role models. Even government officials take their advice on how the country should be run. They are the leaders—the movers and shakers—of the society and the economy.

Dr Manmohan Singh, India's thirteenth prime minister, (who India's business leaders lauded as the father of India's economic reforms of 1991) drew attention to this problem at the annual meeting of CII in May 2007. He expressed concern about the reaction of the have-nots to ostentatious displays of wealth far beyond their reach. He urged business people to help reduce the problems of common Indian citizens. He warned that, otherwise, India's pattern of growth would not be sustainable.

Model 3: Strong leaders—dictators *(Tigers growling; wolves prowling)*

A scenario with 'Tigers Growling and Wolves Prowling' often arises as a reaction to the previous scenarios. Frustrated by perceived injustices and the inability of democratic processes to address them, people will sometimes support dictatorial leaders who claim to take up their cause. This scenario is about the uses and abuses of concentrated power.

The tiger cannot be challenged by other animals and gets his way, while wolves (the tiger's supporters) prey on helpless smaller animals around them. As Lord Acton said, 'Power tends to corrupt, and absolute power corrupts absolutely.' Like wolves in the jungle, the families and friends of powerful leaders often live off commoners who fear them.

Model 4: Leaders of community action *(Fireflies arising)*

The final scenario is fundamentally different. It places the onus for driving change deeper in the system on the ordinary citizens of the country and does not rely on those at the top, unlike the other scenarios. India is a diverse, democratic and complex system, and the theory of 'complex self-adaptive systems' suggests that such a dynamic entity cannot be controlled from a single centre. Change in India will be brought about by many hundreds of thousands of people taking the initiative at a local level, rather than waiting for an all-powerful (and, one hopes, benign) leader to emerge at the centre.

The picture for this scenario is a hot, summer night in the Indian countryside. Fireflies appear in the darkness and, as their numbers increase, the night is aglitter with myriad lights. The fireflies represent Indians from all walks of life who take the first steps towards achieving change in their own lives and in the world around them, thereby inspiring others to do the same.

The fireflies are arising in India. They include the thousands of women running self-help groups, the growing number of social entrepreneurs, the small businesses, the socially responsible corporations and even the government officials who are bringing about change through innovation. They include my young friends who turn to me for advice on how to design their social enterprises.

The number of young people who have set out to change the way India has been developing so far gives me great hope. They have different causes that inspire them—for some it is the improvement of livelihoods of people who have been left behind by the lopsided growth of the economy; for others, it is the inclusion of women, or the education of children of poor parents. They are the 'fireflies'—leaders of change lit up by their internal passion to make a difference.

As Robert F. Kennedy said in a speech in South Africa, at the height of tension in that country:

> It is from nameless acts of courage and belief that the human story is shaped. Each time a man stands up for an idea or acts to improve the lot of others or strikes out against injustice, he sends forth a tiny ripple of hope. And crossing each other from a million different centers of energy and daring those ripples build a current that can sweep aside the mightiest walls of oppression and resistance.

Millions of leaders are required, with millions of small local movements, to improve the world for everyone. The scale must be in the movement of change and the outcomes it produces, not in the size of the organization that makes the change.

LEARNING TO LEARN

The solution clients want from consultants in VUCA times is how to find their own solutions.

VUCA has become a trendy managerial acronym that stands for volatility, uncertainty, complexity and ambiguity. Another popular refrain these days is, 'The only constant is change.'

The boundaries of industries are changing rapidly and unpredictably and so are the basic concepts of industry. The most recent is Industry 4.0. The shape of the economy is also changing radically. Economists were struggling to understand what the shape of the 'new normal' would be even before the Covid pandemic upended the global economy. Before the pandemic, they thought they had only lost their map and could use their compass to guide them. The pandemic has shown them that their compass—their fundamental theories—can no longer show them the way.

The Chinese expression, 'May you live in interesting times', is not a blessing but a curse, some Chinese friends told me, because 'interesting' times in this expression means 'challenging' times. Challenging times can be interesting only if one opens up one's mind to learn.

These are challenging times for teachers and for students of business management. Much of what the teachers know and teach will no longer be relevant. What should they teach students then? The most useful lesson for students to learn is how to learn so that they can keep learning all their lives.

The teachers will have to unlearn many of the fundamental truths they had learnt. They must open their minds to accept new fundamentals of economics and business. It is difficult enough to learn new facts within an accepted framework, but when the framework that provides basic stability must be unlearnt, teachers are compelled to find a new course; without their trusted compass, at that.

Thomas Kuhn, the philosopher and physicist, introduced the term 'paradigm' to describe a structure of thought that has been widely adopted. In his classic treatise, *The Structure of Scientific Revolutions,* he explains why paradigms are hard to change. The reason is, many institutions are founded on the same paradigm and a change in the paradigm will result in shifts of power. Naturally, those in power want to maintain the status quo and not lose their hold; they will resist change and they will defend the present paradigm.

In the world of business management, business management education and business management consulting, the paradigm is 'the business of business must be only business' (which is to make profits), and any change in it seems to be resisted by all.

Chris Argyris, the business theorist and professor emeritus at Harvard Business School, coined the term 'double loop learning'. Single loop learning, he explained, involves improvement of knowledge and practice without changing the underlying theory. Whereas double loop learning questions the validity of the underlying theory and requires adoption of a new theory to produce the desired results. Double loop learning requires a change in paradigm which, as Kuhn explained, is very difficult.

Chris Argyris's most influential book is *Knowledge for Action*. He explains how people in action, as people in business and government are expected to be, must manage their own learning. They must find better ways to apply prevalent theories and learn new theories while they are in action. A good analogy is: they must redesign their aeroplane while they are flying in it. This sounds like a risky proposition but it becomes necessary sometimes. Indeed, business managers and policymakers will have to redesign their mental aeroplanes while they fly in them to shape a more resilient world after Covid.

How can students learn in action and continue to learn all their lives?

Sir Basil H. Liddell Hart, the British military historian, answers this question and gives good advice to young people in his book, *Why Don't We Learn from History?* Military historians provide great insights into learning in action amidst uncertainty.

The sun never set on the British Empire in the nineteenth century. The Union Jack fluttered everywhere around the globe. How did a small island nation create this vast empire? It was the young men in the British Army, the British civil services and Britain's merchant trading firms that formed the backbone of the British Empire. These men were looking for work and adventure, and there were few opportunities in Britain. They were the second or third sons of their parents. While the first inherited the father's lands, peerage or business, the others had to look farther afield.

These young men, working in a faraway land, far from the centre of their government and headquarters of their companies, learnt how to get things done. They rallied troops of local people to fight for them and enrolled the locals to help them collect revenues and taxes, much of it to send home to Britain. How could these young men do it?

Liddell Hart says young officers were told to find a quiet spot, on a hillock or under a tree, before they led their troops into action and write their thoughts down in their notebooks about the situation they were in. What was known to them and what was not? What did they know about the enemy's intentions and resources? What did they want to achieve and what were the resources they could marshal? The lesson that served them well was, reflect on the situation to devise a strategy for action even when the enemy's guns are booming all around you.

Young people are impatient. They want to get on with the task. 'Execution, not strategy', became a mantra for go-getting business leaders since the 1990s. 'Just Do It!' says the popular Nike slogan.

However, it is wise to look before one leaps.

While Liddell Hart advises young leaders to reflect before action, Argyris goes further. He recommends reflection along with action in his book *Knowledge for Action*. In fact, he recommends reflection at two levels: on the scene of action around oneself and on ideas within one's own head.

The young officer on the hillock had many factors to consider, but it seems that young people today must consider many more things simultaneously in whatever they do. They are not only being bombarded with information from all sides but they also have to process the reality that the world is changing around them rapidly.

'The new imperative has become synthesis—the capacity to gather, prune, organize information of all sizes and forms, and *to repeat the cycle indefinitely* [italics mine],' says Howard Gardner, the American developmental psychologist and the John H. and Elisabeth A. Hobbs Research Professor of Cognition and Education at the Harvard Graduate School of Education at Harvard University. In his book, *Truth, Beauty, and Goodness Reframed: Educating for the Virtues in the Twenty-First Century*, he recommends that students should keep journals noting their reflections and their questions. He says, 'If they have accumulated and kept track of their learnings, they can bring a soundness to their judgements.'

'Which combination of virtues is most vital to cherish and pass on? I would single out two,' Gardner says. 'The practical truths of a life that was lived well, and the morals and ethics of a life well served.'

Mahatma Gandhi was a great note-keeper. He listened to his mind and recorded his questions and insights in his notebooks. His autobiography is aptly titled, *The Story of My Experiments with Truth.*

Good teachers must be triple-level learners. Whenever paradigms shift, not only must they learn new techniques to teach but they must also learn new theories. In addition, they must learn how to teach their students how to learn for the rest of their lives.

Good consultants are like teachers. They don't take actions themselves; their clients do. They must learn along with, and perhaps a little ahead of, their clients. They must also learn to change their methods of consulting and help clients to learn faster to find their own solutions, not try to find specific solutions for them.

EPILOGUE

LEARNING TO PLAY THE DRUM

Learning to become a better consultant to help others achieve what they want.

I retired as a consultant in 2008 when I was invited by the then prime minister to serve as a member of the Planning Commission. I resigned as a member in 2014 when the government changed. Later that year, in November, I received a request from some young Indians to help them with something unusual.

They called themselves GAP—Global Action against Poverty. They had an idea for an unusual meeting in the Sabarmati Ashram on 12 March 2015. It was the anniversary of the day Mahatma Gandhi had begun the long Dandi March from the ashram to extract salt from the sea. Thousands of people had joined him as he marched on to claim back from the foreign rulers the people's rights to produce their own salt.

The GAP team had invited Professor Muhammad Yunus, the founder of the Grameen Bank and winner of the Nobel Peace Prize; Elabhen Bhat, founder of the remarkable SEWA organization in India; Bill Drayton, founder of the Asoka Foundation and seven other remarkable persons to the meeting at Sabarmati. The GAP team was proposing to invite 200 others who, like themselves, were already making some efforts to reduce poverty in their surroundings. These change-makers wanted to have more impact, but did not know how.

The GAP team asked me to curate the meeting and extract the 'secret ingredient' these remarkable persons knew and pass it on to the 200 change-makers looking for it. Their aim was to produce more empowered and wiser change-makers who would leave the ashram with clear action plans about how they could bring about a change in the world.

Changing the world is not an engineering exercise, I told them. It cannot be reduced to a series of predetermined mechanical steps. There is an inner journey, within the change-maker, that must be undertaken too. Persons who change the world are like fireflies with an inner light. They are lifelong learners, I suggested, as Mahatma Gandhi was.

The change-makers must be prepared to extract the secret ingredient not only from the great leaders they would meet in the ashram but from within themselves too. They should introspect: What drives them to change the world and what would they need to learn to have more impact in it? I outlined their journey plans; it would be along three tracks: actions, creating new partnerships and learning.

I asked the GAP team to prepare themselves for the meeting. I requested them to think about their own journeys, their own plans and, as their first learning step, to share their stories with each other and with me.

One of them asked me about *my* plans. What did I want to do, now that I was out of the hurly-burly of working within the government? What did I want to learn? Would I learn to play golf now that I would have time for it? It made me think.

I remembered my favourite carol, the 'Little Drummer Boy'. He says he has no wealth to offer to Lord Jesus. All he has is his drum, which he will play for the baby Jesus. His offering is the 'par-rup-a-pum-pum' of his drum, which he will play his very best for the Lord. I want to give *my* best at whatever I do.

When I was in my thirties, I had read the classic book *To Have or to Be?* by philosopher Erich Fromm. He contrasts two ways of living and achieving. One is a striving to have more and the other is a journey to become a better being. I was then in the midst of a challenging project to ensure that my company—an under-resourced Indian company that had ventured into foreign waters—could beat the biggest and the best of the world in a foreign market in which the others were already entrenched. I was the designated leader. We did beat them and achieve our goal.

Fromm stirred many questions in me. What was my role in this achievement? Did I deserve credit for it? As I have grown older, which is inevitable, I have been drawn to the ancient Indian wisdom of adjusting one's work to the stages of one's life. In the 'householder' stage, spanning the middle of one's life, one produces offspring, generates wealth to support them and strives for achievements (while following the Gita's dictum of the right to the work and not the fruits). That stage passes with age and another comes by when one must give up those pursuits to reflect on who one is, and concentrate on becoming a better being.

I have asked myself many times in my life, when I have paused to reflect, what kind of work do I aspire to do well? The answer came, softly at first and more assuredly now, that I want to help others to work collectively so that they can produce the results they want. I want to play the drum. Provide the rhythm in the background that enables others to coordinate their music. And I want to play it well.

The percussionist—the drummer or the tabla player—does not play the melody nor sing the song. When many instruments are being played and many voices are singing, the percussion enables them to play and sing in unison to the same rhythm.

I have sung songs and sung them well, too, when I was in that phase of my life, when it was my role to be the singer. I have done my fifty years. Now others must sing and play, and I will provide them with rhythm, if they want it, to help them perform better while they are on the stage. My aspiration now is to be a better drummer and a better human being.

My action plan is to assist those who need a drummer. How should a drummer measure his success? Is it by the large number of concerts he has played in, or is it by the quality of the concerts, even if they were very few? At this stage in my life, when time is running out, as it inevitably does, it is quality not quantity that I aspire for.

My collaboration plan is to be selective about who I engage with. I must be selective because time is scarce and there is none to waste. I must engage with those who really want a drummer; not because it is customary for them to have one but because they know that without a drummer they cannot achieve what they want to.

My learning plan is to learn to restrain myself from wasting my time on what is popular and what brings only a passing fame and to also learn to say 'No' to the greed for popularity, for approbation and for more followers.

I must be better. I must learn the dynamics within the ensembles of players and singers—what makes it difficult for them to coordinate with each other and what would enable them to play harmoniously together to produce the music that will uplift the world. I want to play the drum better and be a better consultant to those who are changing the world to make it a better place for everyone.